THE UNIVERSITY OF MICHIGAN

CENTER FOR SOUTH AND SOUTHEAST ASIAN STUDIES

MICHIGAN PAPERS ON SOUTH AND SOUTHEAST ASIA

Ann Arbor, Michigan
USA

THE PHILIPPINE ECONOMY AND THE UNITED STATES

STUDIES IN PAST AND PRESENT INTERACTIONS

edited by

Norman G. Owen

Ann Arbor
The University of Michigan
Center for South and Southeast Asian Studies

Michigan Papers on South and Southeast Asia

Number 22

1983

Library of Congress Catalog Card Number: 82-74314

ISBN 0-89148-024-2 (cloth)
ISBN 0-89148-025-0 (paper)

Publication of this volume was made possible
in part by financial assistance from the Luce
Fund for Asian Studies and the Business and
International Education Program, Center for
South and Southeast Asian Studies, The
University of Michigan.

Printed in the United States of America

CONTENTS

CONTRIBUTORS

FRANK H. GOLAY is Professor Emeritus of Economics and Asian
Studies at Cornell University, where he has also served as
Director of the Southeast Asia Program, the Philippines
Project, and the London-Cornell Project. His publications
include *The Philippines: Public Policy and National Economic
Development*, *The United States and the Philippines* (editor
and coauthor), and *Underdevelopment and Economic Nationalism
in Southeast Asia* (editor and coauthor), as well as many
articles on economics and economic history.

GRANT K. GOODMAN is Professor of History at the University
of Kansas, Lawrence. He is a specialist in both Japanese
and Philippine history. Among his publications on the
Philippines are *Davao: A Case Study in Philippine-Japanese
Relations*, *Four Aspects of Philippine-Japanese Relations,
1930-1940*, and, most recently, *From Bataan to Tokyo: Diary
of a Filipino Student in Wartime Japan, 1943-44*.

HAROLD C. LIVESAY received his Ph.D. in economic and
business history from The Johns Hopkins University.
Currently he is Professor of History and chairman of the
History Department at Virginia Polytechnic Institute. Among
his numerous publications are *American Made: Men Who Built
the American Economic Tradition*, *Samuel Gompers and
Organized Labor in America*, and *Andrew Carnegie and the Rise
of Big Business*.

VICTOR M. ORDOÑEZ, currently Senior Ministerial Adviser to the Ministry of Trade, Republic of the Philippines, is on leave from De La Salle University, where he has served as Dean of the Graduate School of Business and Education and Director of the Educational Management Center, and from the Bancom Group of Companies, where he was vice-president and managing director of the Bancom Institute of Development Technology. He holds seven academic degrees, including the Ph.D., from Philippine colleges and universities, and has pursued postdoctoral studies in the United States. He has written extensively on project management, rural development, international education, and the role of private enterprise in developing countries.

NORMAN G. OWEN studied the history of Southeast Asia at the School of Oriental and African Studies (University of London) and at the University of Michigan, from which he received his Ph.D. His publications include *Compadre Colonialism: Studies on the Philippines Under American Rule* (editor and coauthor) and *Prosperity Without Progress: Manila Hemp and Material Life in the Colonial Philippines* (forthcoming). He is currently a Research Fellow in the Department of Pacific and Southeast Asian History, Research School of Pacific Studies, The Australian National University.

ROBERT T. SNOW graduated from Swarthmore College and holds a Ph.D. from Harvard University. In his dissertation he examined the impact of the Philippine export-processing zone on the new work force which it created. He spent three years as a Research Associate at the East-West Center, Honolulu, studying the social and cultural effects of transnational corporations. He is currently a Social Science Researcher with the Research and Planning Department of the Maryknoll Fathers, Maryknoll, New York.

PREFACE

A dozen years ago, when American interest and academic investment in Southeast Asia were at their height, a remarkable number of students of the Philippines were enrolled at the University of Michigan. Once a week several of us met for a seminar at the home of Professor David Joel Steinberg, and there we learned about the history of Philippine-American relations, not just from him, but from each other. We were not mature professionals, but we had access to some remarkably good collections of printed and manuscript sources on the Philippines, and we were led by a first-rate scholar and teacher who encouraged us to regard each other as colleagues rather than rivals. The result was an experience from which we all benefited.

Selected papers from that seminar were later revised and published as *Compadre Colonialism*.* In the introduction to that volume I noted in the papers certain "recurrent themes and mutual presuppositions" that "reflect[ed] in part the similarities in the academic experience of the authors, in part our interaction with each other." Thus, despite some differences in our interpretations of Philippine history it was possible to speak of an "underlying consensus," which was reflected in the title of the volume.

---

*Norman G. Owen, ed., *Compadre Colonialism: Studies on the Philippines Under American Rule*, Michigan Papers on South and Southeast Asia, no. 3 (Ann Arbor: The University of Michigan, Center for South and Southeast Asian Studies, 1971).

By the late 1970s the United States was turning its back on Southeast Asia and "area centers" were no longer expanding, but fighting to hold on to what they had. At this juncture the Luce Fund for Asian Studies entered the picture, supporting with substantial grants various projects for the study of interactions between Asia and the United States. One of these grants was awarded to the University of Michigan for the study of "U.S.-Philippine Interactions as Reflected in Oral Histories," a project which included the reestablishment of a regular colloquium.

Each fall term, from 1977 through 1979, we met on Friday afternoons to discuss Philippine-American interactions. This time, however, we were not limited to a handful of graduate and undergraduate students pooling their ignorance and striving to rise above it. Thanks to the Luce Fund we were able to supplement faculty and student presentations with guest speakers brought in from all over the United States; at times we even caught visitors from the Philippines who happened to be passing through the Midwest. The result was something of a cross between a lecture series and a seminar, with "imported" experts introducing new material, resident scholars (Karl Hutterer, Michael Cullinane, and myself) attempting to provide context and continuity, and other faculty and students asking the questions which stimulated discussion.

We deliberately chose to cast our net widely. Besides political history (the central theme of *Compadre Colonialism*), we touched on economics, linguistics, literature, photography, and art, anything, in fact, that might be covered by the rubric "U.S.-Philippine Interactions." Some speakers offered us polished prose or chapters of books enroute to publication, while others presented rough first drafts of preliminary outlines of tentative hypotheses; we welcomed them all. We made no effort to impose arbitrary order on this magnificent diversity of approaches and evidence; instead, we told the students that each of them--each of us--was responsible for discovering or establishing his or her own linkages among the papers.

For all those able to attend it regularly, the colloquium was an unqualified success. But that number was necessarily limited, so we felt we ought to make the best of the papers available to a wider audience. A canvass of the participants produced, as might be expected, a wide diversity of responses to this suggestion. From the papers that eventually were submitted we selected for publication those which dealt with the topic stated in the title of this volume, *The Philippine Economy and the United States: Studies in Past and Present Interactions*. Beyond this common topic, however, the reader will discern no such "underlying consensus" as was found in *Compadre Colonialism*. The authors do not share the same "academic experience," nor, more significantly, did they all interact with each other in this colloquium, rubbing the rough corners off their divergent views. I am the only one among them to have heard all the others, and though my paper here benefits from what they have taught me, it does not represent their individual or collective views. It is not, as the introduction to *Compadre Colonialism* purported to be, my "sense of the meeting," for no such "meeting" of the authors ever occurred.

Instead, readers of this volume will be aware of contradictions, of debate, even of fundamentally irreconcilable views. While none of the authors regards the American connection as totally advantageous to the Philippine economy, there is considerable difference between those who regard it as generally significant and malign and those who suggest that it was less consequential than has been believed and more neutral, or even beneficial, in its effects. There are, of course, important policy implications in this difference. The former perspective suggests that the best course for the Philippines in the future would be to put a greater distance between the two economies, while the latter is at least compatible with efforts to increase mutual trade and investment. But, though these perspectives have political implications, the argument on both sides is free of overt ideology. Each of us has, I believe, made an honest effort to come to terms with the difficult question of what the "special relationship" really means in the economic sphere, and it is the honesty of that effort that makes the argument worth following.

Another recurrent, though less explicit, theme permeating these papers is that of the relationship between government and private business. Of particular concern here is the political role of American enterprises in the Philippines, in their relations with both Washington and Manila. Clearly these firms have always attempted to influence both capitals; equally clearly they have not always got what they wanted. But were they generally successful, suffering only occasional and peripheral defeats, or were they essentially inconsequential, a secondary factor in shaping the economic policy of both countries? If the latter, what other interests outweighed them, to what ends? Conversely, how much have official policies emanating from either Manila or Washington dictated the nature and operations of American business in the Philippines? Has Filipino enterprise profited from "economic nationalism" or can it also flourish under a more open trade and investment regime? Does public policy shape capitalism, or is it the other way around? Though few of the papers address these questions directly, all bear on them in one way or another and thus contribute to the ongoing debate over Philippine-American economic interactions.

What we share, finally, is a feeling that these questions are important and a scholarly commitment to explore them with full respect for their complexities and ambiguities. We offer these papers to readers with the same admonition we gave to students in the colloquium: it is up to you to evaluate these conflicting views and reach what resolution you can.

ACKNOWLEDGMENTS

We acknowledge first of all our gratitude to the
generosity of the Luce Fund for Asian Studies, without which
the colloquium would never have taken place. Among
participants in the colloquium whose papers are not included
in this volume we would like to single out Karl Hutterer and
Michael Cullinane (who administered the grant and chaired
the colloquium), as well as Ronald K. Edgerton, Morton J.
Netzorg, Bernardito Operario, Joel E. Rocamora and Aram A.
Yengoyan, each of whom added to our general sense of how the
economic interaction worked. We would also like to
acknowledge the many contributors to the colloquium who
addressed themselves to noneconomic aspects of Philippine-
American interactions, work no less worthy for not being
appropriate for publication in this volume. As we moved
toward publication we benefited from the official labors of
Janet Opdyke (Publications Editor, Center for South and
Southeast Asian Studies) and the unofficial labors of
Michael Cullinane and Roberta Y. Owen. Financial assistance
in the later stages was provided by the Business and
International Education Program of the Center for South and
Southeast Asian Studies. Finally, I would like to thank all
my coauthors for their patience. Most of the papers were
first given in 1978-79 and revised no later than 1980; a
part of the responsibility for the delay in their
publication must be mine.

Norman G. Owen

"MANILA AMERICANS" AND PHILIPPINE POLICY:
THE VOICE OF AMERICAN BUSINESS

Frank H. Golay

I

When William Howard Taft, a young federal district
court judge, was asked by President McKinley in January 1900
to join the Philippine Commission which would provide civil
government for the new colony, Taft told the president that
he opposed taking the colony and was satisfied with his lot
as a federal judge.[1] After some hesitation Taft agreed to
serve as head of the commission and quickly gravitated to
the imperialist mainstream of the Republican Party. Taft
and his colleagues on the commission were busy during their
first year in the Philippine Islands concocting ambitious
plans for the colony. They were challenged to succeed as
colonial administrators and the tasks they faced were
formidable and stretched into the distant future.

McKinley enjoined the commission to extend free primary
education over the Philippines and to blanket the colony
with municipal governments which would serve as the
principal vehicle for tutoring Filipinos in self-rule.[2] If
the colony was to be retained indefinitely, Filipino
nationalism, which was in fever heat at the turn of the
century, would have to be dampened by a colonial government
capable of winning the loyalty of Filipinos by improving
governmental services and by raising the material well-being
of Filipinos generally. To meet these goals, the colonial

1

government would require financial resources and the
commission promptly turned to the task of devising a tax
structure that would generate the funds needed. The
commissioners also realized that continuation of American
rule would depend on their success in getting the moribund
Philippine economy moving, as taxes would generate needed
revenues only if economic growth was maintained. To
facilitate this process, the commission laid down ambitious
plans for systems of roads and railroads, improvements in
port facilities, and other public works.

Because they envisaged a prolonged period of colonial
rule and were keenly aware of the underlying ambivalence
with which Americans generally viewed the imperial
enterprise, the commissioners recognized the need to create
constituencies of Americans in the Philippines with a stake
in indefinite retention of the colony. To do so, they
assigned priority to making Manila over into a healthy,
attractive, and comfortable city with an efficient
administration providing the amenities found in American
cities. Similar priority was assigned to a "hill station,"
or summer capital, to which Americans could flee the
debilitating heat and humidity of Manila.

One body of Americans that never questioned the probity
of American rule or the need to retain the colony
indefinitely was the American component of the colonial
bureaucracy, particularly career administrators at the
higher levels. These Americans were paid well and lived
well and they were assiduous in denigrating the capability
of Filipinos to govern. By doing so they satisfied
themselves that American rule must continue.

In their first report to Washington after six months in
the colony, the commissioners urged that the friars, the
Spanish priests of the Catholic missionary orders who
comprised the principal instrument of direct rule under
Spain, be replaced by Americans, and this changeover was

completed in the early years of the century.[3] American
priests were not numerous, but once the Church hierarchy in
the Philippines was Americanized, the prelate in Manila and
the regional bishops had the ears of Church leaders in
America, which amplified the voice of this constituency with
a stake in continued American rule. Although relatively few
in number, Protestant missionaries also magnified their
contribution to retention by enlisting the American churches
that supported them behind the cause.

Another constituency supporting retention was the
officer corps of the United States Army. Starved for funds
following the Civil War, the army shrank in size until at
the outbreak of war with Spain it numbered twenty-seven
thousand officers and men. Those following a career in the
officer corps endured long periods without promotion while
confined to isolated posts scattered over the American West.
They were abruptly released from their thralldom by the war,
which saw the army balloon fourfold to one hundred thousand
officers and men, a level from which it did not recede
thereafter. The contribution of the war with Spain and the
Filipino-American War to their welfare and social status
created a mystique or outlook shared by members of the
officer corps which ensured that this body of Americans
would support continuation of American rule.

The American constituency that Taft and his colleagues
counted on to provide the core of support for indefinite
retention was expected to materialize and flourish as
American capital and enterprise migrated to the new colony.
To ensure that this American interest would grow, the
commission promptly turned to the task of devising a
development strategy which would enhance the attractiveness
of the colony as an outlet for American investment.

II

Although one-sixth of Philippine exports were shipped
to the United States in the 1890s, when Americans in the
expeditionary army arrived in the islands at the turn of the
century they found few compatriots. The voice of the
business community in Manila, which controlled the import
trade of the colony as well as the organization of
production, assembly, and marketing of major export crops
and the provision of interisland shipping services, was
provided by the Manila Merchants Association (MMA), in which
British interests were dominant. Smaller chambers of
commerce comprising national groups of businessmen existed,
but their role was more social than economic. Sugar
producers, predominantly Filipinos of mixed Filipino-Spanish
and Filipino-Chinese heritage, were organized into
influential pressure groups centered in Iloilo on Panay and
on the island of Negros. Tobacco merchants and cigar
manufacturers, concentrated in Manila and including a
spectrum of nationalities, were organized and vocal.
Finally, there was the Hispanicized and active Economic
Society of Friends of the Country, which bridged officials
in the colonial administration, *ilustrado* intellectuals, and
businessmen of diverse nationality.[4]

As American control was extended over the islands,
McKinley was ruling the Philippines under his war powers.
With the exchange of ratifications of the Treaty of Paris in
April 1899, however, the Constitution vested Congress with
the power to make all "needful rules" for governing the
colony and to decide upon its ultimate disposition.
Encouraged by Republican gains in the 56th Congress,
convened in December 1899, Secretary of War Elihu Root, who
was responsible for the administration of the new colony
under military government, drafted legislation calling upon
Congress to delegate its constitutional power to govern the
colony to a civil government appointed by the president. To

4

reassure Congress and hasten passage of the measure, McKinley announced his appointments to the Philippine Commission, which would take over administration of the colony. Root's measure, introduced by Senator John Spooner (Wisc.), proved controversial, and the Spooner bill could not be brought to a vote.[5]

The election of 1900, which William Jennings Bryan, the Democratic candidate, insisted on fighting on the "paramount issue" of imperialism, produced a substantial victory for McKinley, which Republicans generally interpreted as a mandate to rule the Philippines indefinitely. Encouraged by the election, Taft and his colleagues urged Root to try again to obtain from Congress a grant of power which would enable the commission to initiate development of the stagnant island economy. Shortly after the election the commission reported to Root that "sufficient applications to purchase public lands have been received to know that large amounts of American capital are only waiting the opportunity to invest" and proposed "that congressional authority be vested in the government of the islands to adopt a proper public land system and to sell land on proper terms."[6]

The legislative docket of the short session of the outgoing Congress was crowded with priority bills, however, and Root took no steps to revive the Spooner measure until early in January when the commission cabled:

> Passage of Spooner bill at present session
> greatly needed to secure best results from
> improving conditions. Until its passage no
> purely central civil government can be
> established, no substantial investments of
> private capital in internal improvements
> possible. . . . Sale of public lands and
> allowance of mining claims impossible until
> Spooner bill. Hundreds of American miners

on ground awaiting law to perfect claims,
more coming.[7]

At this point, Root attached a modified version of the
Spooner bill as an amendment to the army appropriation bill
which was before the Senate. When the Spooner amendment
came up in the Senate, Democratic opponents of Republican
colonial policy launched a filibuster to keep the measure
from coming to a vote. Facing defeat, Republican leaders of
the Senate amended the measure to emasculate the authority
requested by the commission in order to obtain passage of
the army appropriation bill.[8]

Aware that opponents of retention were determined to
prevent a blanket delegation of Congress's power to govern
the colony to the Philippine Commission, the McKinley
administration made plans to introduce a draft organic law,
or constitution, for the colony in the new 57th Congress.
Meanwhile, the commission would have to govern the
Philippines under the president's restricted war powers.
The day following adjournment of Congress in 1901, Root
instructed the commission to recommend provisions to be
included in the government measure.[9]

Concerned to get the island economy moving after four
years of rebellion, war, and economic dislocation, the
commission urged Congress to allow American enterprise and
capital to play a major role in developing the colony. The
commission proposed that the migration of these resources be
induced by permitting American investors liberal access to
public lands and mineral and forest resources; by empowering
the commission to charter corporations and grant franchises
on liberal terms; by permitting the commission to sell bonds
in the United States to raise money to build ports, roads,
and other public works; by amending the National Banking Act
to permit American banks to operate in the Philippines; and
by granting imports from the colony a substantial and
nonreciprocal reduction in the American tariff.[10]

The partisan split in Congress over Philippine policy was conspicuous in the acrimonious debates in 1902 and the rough treatment given the commission's development strategy. The Payne Tariff Act of 1902 established a nonreciprocal tariff preference of 25 percent for imports from the colony and provided that duties collected on Philippine commodities would be turned over to the insular government. This concession proved meaningless, however, as Republican administrations since 1860 had raised the wall of American protection to such a high level that even a preference of 25 percent left duties that excluded most Philippine products. The Organic Act of 1902 limited the authority of the colonial government to sell bonds in the United States to finance "public improvements" at $5 million, a level not changed for fourteen years despite repeated pleas from the commission for increases. Congress ignored the banking recommendation of the commission and established stringent limits on access by individuals and corporations to public land and other natural resources which severely limited the role played by American capital and enterprise in the development of plantations, mines, and forest industries. Although every subsequent report of the commission repeated basic recommendations made in 1901, they received little attention from Congress.[11]

With their initial development strategy a shambles, Taft and his colleagues decided to concentrate their efforts on obtaining a larger trade preference for the colony. Taft returned to the States in 1904 to succeed Root as Secretary of War, a position from which he could dominate American Philippine policy as he worked for a larger tariff preference for the Philippines. Taft made no effort to conceal the purpose of his crusade. He was now a confirmed retentionist and assumed that this position was shared generally by Americans. In repeated speeches in the colony, in testimony before congressional committees, and in

7

speeches on behalf of Roosevelt's candidacy in 1904, he
spread the message:

> If we bring them behind the tariff wall, if
> they see that association with the United
> States is beneficial to them, as I verily
> believe it will be, it is unlikely they will
> desire full independence.[12]

Thanks to Theodore Roosevelt's decisions not to seek
reelection and to support Taft as his successor, Taft
captured the presidency in 1908. He emphasized tariff
reform in his campaign and upon taking office he called
Congress into special session to revise the tariff. Taft
also was prepared to use the leverage that was his as newly
elected president to obtain the tariff preference he wanted
for the colony. He used this leverage to reach a
"gentleman's agreement" under which Republican leaders of
Congress agreed to support a measure making mutual trade
between the United States and the colony free of duty. In
return, Taft accepted liberal absolute quotas on Philippine
shipments of sugar, cigar tobacco, and cigars. With passage
of the Payne-Aldrich tariff in 1909, Taft reached the goal
for which he had struggled for eight years.[13] The colony
now had a development strategy which ensured economic
expansion and containment of Filipino nationalism and
promised an influential constituency of Americans supporting
indefinite retention.

The eight years required to reach agreement on a
development strategy for the colony saw American enterprise
and capital in the Philippines grow slowly. During the
three years, 1892-1894, trade with the United States
accounted for 3 percent of Philippine imports and 16 percent
of exports. These ratios gradually increased over the first
decade of American rule until, for the three years
1907-1909, trade with the United States accounted for
28 percent of insular exports and 18 percent of imports.

American businessmen in the Philippines were not interested in this trade as producers of export commodities, but as merchants assembling exports and as importers and wholesalers of less than one-fifth of the colony's imports.[14] As a result, American businessmen in the Philippines played a minor lobbying role as development policy was forged in Congress.

An American Chamber of Commerce (ACC) was formed in Manila as early as the late fall of 1901 when Congress was preparing to write an organic law for the colony. In December the chamber cabled McKinley urging "free entry of Philippine products, especially raw materials." The new ACC also joined with other chambers of commerce and trade associations in the Philippines to send Brewster Cameron to Washington to lobby for the largest possible nonreciprocal tariff preference for insular products. When Congress limited the preference to twenty-five cents, Manila Americans organized a mass meeting, of unknown mass, and passed a resolution protesting the disappointing preference.[15]

In anticipation of the more important Organic Act, the chamber adopted "A Memorial to Congress Suggesting Needed Legislation for the Philippine Islands," which called for the "sale and settlement" of public lands in the colony, providing access to mineral resources, "facilitating the cutting of timber on the public domain and the granting of franchises for the development of the islands and their resources," extension of American coastwise shipping policy to the colony, establishment of mutual free trade, and the admission of "coolie labor," as "native labor is inadequate and insufficient for the development of the islands."[16]

Following its lobbying efforts in 1902, the chamber lapsed into inactivity, although it continued to exist for a few years. The basic weakness of the chamber as the voice of American business in the colony is not hard to understand. American enterprise and capital played a minor role in the laggard economic development of the Philippines over the first decade of American rule. Through the sale of bonds in the United States, the savings of Americans were flowing to the insular government and to the Manila Railroad Company and the Philippine Railway Company, which were constructing lines in the colony. The Manila Electric Railway and Lighting Company (MERALCO), operating street railways and supplying electric power to Manila and its environs, was prospering. These investments amounted to $44 million and accounted for 63 percent of all American investment in the colony in mid-1911. Most numerous were smaller American enterprises engaged in commerce, general contracting, operation of livery stables and garages, and simple manufacturing, largely in Manila. There were sixty-eight of these firms representing American investment of $10.5 million. Only one firm engaged in constructing public works accounted for American investment of as much as $1 million. Investments in "farms and plantations," mines, and lumbering accounted for $11.3 million of American investment, but, with the exception of the unprofitable San Jose sugar plantation and sugar mill on Mindoro Island, none of these enterprises represented investment of as much as $1 million. The remaining $5 million of American investment was scattered over holdings of urban real estate, one bank, several newspapers, restaurants, and other enterprises.[17]

Shortly after he joined the commission as Secretary of Commerce and Police in 1904, W. Cameron Forbes gave a reception for ACC members and afterwards recorded in his journal: "These Americans, some of whom were army sutlers, liquor dealers and others of less noble trades as well as some very good ones . . . have been very touchy because the government didn't pay any attention to them."[18] It was not long after this that the chamber disappeared.

Inasmuch as American enterprises engaged in production, assembly, and shipment of exports were few and small in scale, they played a minor role in Taft's crusade for enlargement of the colony's tariff preference. In extensive hearings on the Curtis bill of 1905, the Payne tariff preference bill of 1906, and the Payne-Aldrich tariff of 1909, and in hearings before the congressional party in the Philippines in 1905, the American voices supporting enlargement of the colony's tariff preference were those of Taft, officials in the colonial administration, and senior officials in the Bureau of Insular Affairs.[19]

United behind the Republican policy of indefinite retention, the commission remained concerned for the weakness of the voice of American business in the colony. As the United States share in insular trade increased, Americans became more active in the Manila Merchants Association until in 1907 the commission initiated a sizable annual subvention to the association to disseminate information in the United States on economic opportunities in the Philippines. During the special tariff session convened by Taft, the MMA distributed widely in the United States a pamphlet extolling "Reciprocal Trade." After passage of the Payne-Aldrich tariff, ten thousand copies of a pamphlet designed "to arouse interest in the possibilities presented in the Philippine Islands for investment of capital and for trade" were distributed abroad. It is unlikely, however, that the MMA was the voice of American business in the islands so much as it was a publicity vehicle for the insular government. When President Wilson Filipinized the commission following his election in 1912, the association's subvention was quickly terminated.[20]

Establishment of mutual free trade in 1909 was followed four years later by passage of the Underwood-Simmons tariff, which removed quantitative restrictions on Philippine shipments to the United States.[21] A year later World War I

erupted and the island economy was launched on a prolonged
period of economic growth. By 1920, the value of imports
into the colony from the United States reached ₱185 million,
a seventeenfold increase over the average level of imports
during the three years, 1907-1909. Insular exports to the
United States also peaked in 1920 at ₱210 million, a
ninefold increase over the average level of such exports
during 1907-1909. Over the three years ending with 1921,
trade with the United States accounted for two-thirds of
insular imports and three-fifths of exports.

With the economy booming, little need was felt by
Manila Americans--in or out of government--to change
economic aspects of colonial policy, and the lobbying
activities of American business interests were sporadic and
of little consequence. Although Manila Americans were
content with the economic relationship, following the
election of Wilson they faced for the first time the threat
of independence. The Democratic platform in 1912 condemned
"the experiment in imperialism as an inexcusable blunder
which has involved us in enormous expense, brought us
weakness instead of strength," and committed the party to
"an immediate declaration of the Nation's purpose to
recognize the independence of the Philippine Islands as soon
as a stable government can be established."[22]

After the Democrats organized the House following the
congressional elections of 1910, Congressman William A.
Jones (Va.) introduced a bill scheduling independence in
1921. Although the Jones measure did not come up in the
regular session of the 62d congress, it was reported by the
Committee on Insular Affairs in 1912 and was available for
consideration in the lame duck session following the
elections of that year. The "Philippine question" played no
significant role in the election, which encouraged Manila
Americans to believe that Wilson would not move abruptly
toward independence. This assessment changed in late

12

December when Wilson returned to his birthplace in Virginia
for a speech in which he declared: "The Philippines are at
present our frontier but I hope we presently are to deprive
ourselves of that frontier." Cameron Forbes reports that
Wilson's words "settled down like a wet, cold blanket over
the merchants and people concerned with the development of
the industry of the islands." Only two months remained
before the 62d Congress expired, however, and Manila
Americans could only endure the threat of the first Jones
bill, which did not come to a vote.[23]

Following his inauguration, Wilson convened a special
session of the 63d Congress to write a new tariff, enact a
personal income tax, establish the Federal Trade Commission,
and create the Federal Reserve System, which left no time
for the "Philippine question." Meanwhile, Congressman Jones
introduced a second bill to move the colonial government to
a new stage of enlarged Filipino autonomy, which included a
preamble promising independence when the Filipinos
demonstrated the ability to maintain a stable government.
The regular session of the 63d Congress was cluttered with
priority legislation, however, and there was little prospect
that the second Jones bill would reach the floor. By late
spring of 1914, it became evident that the House was far
ahead of the Senate in disposing of pressing legislation,
and its Democratic leaders decided to take up Jones's bill.
After two weeks of debate, the bill passed the House with
the preamble intact, but the Senate did not act on the
measure in the closing weeks of the session.[24]

With the bill passed by the House and before the
Senate, the Committee on the Philippines convened hearings
on the bill. Taft and various members of the Philippine
Commission under the Republicans were out in force to oppose
the measure. Manila Americans were represented by two
journalists--Martin Egan and Israel Putnam--who opposed the
bill, and a coterie of American businessmen in Manila

informed the Secretary of War of their opposition by cable.
The bill was reported by the committee, but it proved
impossible to bring it before the Senate in the remaining
days of the 63d Congress.[25]

It was clear to knowledgeable observers that Congress
was disposed to deal with the "Philippine question" in the
new 64th Congress and the Senate committee convened hearings
late in 1915 on a bill introduced by Senator Gilbert
Hitchcock (Neb.) which was modeled on the second Jones bill.
Before reporting the Hitchcock measure, the Senate committee
watered down the promise of independence in the preamble
until it was meaningless and greatly strengthened the
American executive in the new stage of government the bill
provided for the colony. When the measure came before the
Senate, there was widespread unhappiness among Democrats
over the preamble. Republican partisans seized upon the
discomfort of their Democratic colleagues to taunt them for
their failure to carry out the promise of their party's 1912
platform to declare America's purpose to give independence
to the colony. This situation changed abruptly when Senator
James Clarke (Ark.) submitted an early independence
amendment to the bill.   After conferring with Wilson,
Clarke modified his amendment and the president endorsed the
measure. The Clarke amendment was added to the Hitchcock
bill by the vote of the vice-president when the Senate
divided equally on the amendment. Shortly thereafter, the
amended bill was approved by the Senate.[26]

There was no input from representatives of Manila
Americans in the hearings on the Hitchcock bill, but,
following passage of the bill by the Senate,
William N. Kinkaid, a lawyer active in Democratic Party
politics in the Philippines, hurried to Washington to oppose
the Hitchcock bill on behalf of the Catholic Church
hierarchy in the colony and various business clients. The
Manila Merchants Association also got into the act by

passing a resolution petitioning Congress and President
Wilson to postpone legislative action on the "Philippine
question" until the end of the war in Europe.[27]

The Clarke amendment was deleted from the Hitchcock
bill by the House when twenty-six Democrats, most of Irish
extraction from metropolitan constituencies and virtually
all Catholics, refused to abide by the decision of their
party's caucus to support the Clarke amendment.
Subsequently, the House substituted the second Jones bill,
with its promise of independence in the preamble, and it was
approved by the Senate. Having passed the Jones Law, which
moved the colony to a new stage of colonial government,
Congress virtually ignored the "Philippine question" for six
years.

III

The wartime boom sustained economic expansion in the
Philippines and submerged the American-Filipino tensions so
evident during Wilson's first administration. Within a year
the United States was at war and Filipinos generally made it
their war as well, which contributed to social stability and
moderated racial tension in the colony.

The economic expansion of the war years also threatened
trouble. Expenditures on imports for both consumption and
investment were growing and threatened to exceed export
earnings if expansion should falter. The extension of bank
credit, particularly by the rapidly growing, government-
owned Philippine National Bank (PNB), supported investment
in new productive capacity but it also fueled inflation
which promised to encroach on the prosperity enjoyed by the
colony. The extent of economic dislocation attending rapid
expansion was brought home to Americans and Filipinos in
1919, when expenditures abroad raced ahead of foreign
exchange earnings, and insular currency reserves drained
away. A major portion of the reserves were on deposit with

the PNB, but, when they were needed to defend the value of
the peso, it was discovered that the bank's assets--loans to
build sugar and coconut-oil mills--had become illiquid. If
forced to replenish the currency reserves, the PNB would
have been thrown into bankruptcy, which would have magnified
the crisis in the colony.

Revelation of mismanagement of the PNB and the currency
reserves initiated a wave of criticism of Filipino
capabilities for self-government by insular Americans. More
corrosive of racial harmony was the rampant inflation. The
rising cost of living eroded the purchasing power of wages
and salaries, and a series of strikes, a number of them
against American firms, were attended by sporadic violence.

The economic stress occasioned by the end of the war
was embarrassing to the insular government and heightened
tension between Filipinos and Americans. The island economy
appeared to be weathering the economic transition to a
peaceful world, however, when it was hit by the worldwide
slump in commodity prices in the summer of 1920. During the
last half of that year, the weighted index of the prices of
major agricultural commodities of the colony fell by more
than one-half and bottomed out in October 1921 at only one-
third the level of fifteen months earlier. As a result,
earnings from exports in 1921 fell to only 58 percent of the
previous year. Once the currency reserves were exhausted,
the insular treasury could only suspend the sale of dollars
and allow the value of the peso to fall. As the peso sagged
in value, criticism by Manila Americans of the colonial
administration under Governor General Francis B. Harrison
became shrill.[28]

The election of 1920 produced a landslide victory for
the Republicans. In his annual message to the outgoing
Congress a month later, President Wilson reported that the
Filipinos had maintained a stable government and concluded
that "it is now our liberty and our duty to keep our promise

16

to the people of those islands by granting them the independence they so honorably covet."[29] His message fell on deaf ears. The Republicans had no doubt that colonial rule under the Democrats had demonstrated Filipino ineptitude for self-government, and President-elect Harding was busy with plans to send a special investigating mission to the islands to expose the derelictions of Harrison and his Nacionalista Party collaborators.

The political changes under way in the States and the promise of more to come stimulated a burst of activity by the American business community in the Philippines. Americans and their enterprises had flourished during the wartime boom as producers, processors, and exporters of Philippine commodities and as importers and distributors of American products. Insular trade with the United States, which represented less than one-quarter of Philippine trade when mutual free trade was initiated in 1909, accounted for two-thirds of insular trade in 1920. As the American economic stake grew, it was felt more intensely, and the return of the Republicans to power at home was perceived by Americans in the colony as an opportunity to settle the "Philippine question" once and for all. To seize this opportunity, a new American Chamber of Commerce was brought into existence in June 1920 to amplify and focus the voice of American business in the colony.

Harding's nomination in 1920 promised an active Philippine policy which further encouraged the initiative of the American business community. Elected to the Senate in 1914, Harding succeeded to the chairmanship of the Committee on the Philippines when the Republicans organized the Senate in 1919 and was expected to maintain an interest in insular affairs. For many Americans in the colony, his nomination confirmed that the time was opportune to remove the uncertainty which clouded the future relationship between the Philippines and the United States.

To capitalize on this consensus, the *Manila Times*,
recently acquired by George H. Fairchild, an American active
in modernizing the insular sugar industry during the wartime
boom, proposed that "the Philippine Islands should be made a
territory of the United States and that full American
citizenship be granted to Filipinos." The *Times* invited the
American community to rally behind this proposition, and a
few days later virtually the entire membership of the new
American Chamber of Commerce endorsed a resolution calling
for establishment of a "territorial government under the
sovereignty of the United States."[30] Throughout the
continental expansion of the United States, establishment of
a territorial government by Congress had been the first step
in a process culminating in the admission of a territory to
the Union as a state or states. Territorial status had been
granted to Hawaii. Why shouldn't the Philippines receive
the same treatment?

The agitation by Americans for territorial status was
welcome to many influential Filipinos, some because they
were annexationists at heart and others because they longed
for an American protectorate and assurance that duty-free
access to the American market would continue. As a result,
Filipino opposition to the territorial-status campaign was
muted, which encouraged the campaign's organizers. The
enthusiasm of Manila Americans for their new crusade also
was encouraged by a parade of senators and congressmen who
junketed to the colony following adjournment of Congress in
1920, affording opportunities for spokesmen of the American
community to make their case for territorial status.

The movement for territorial status peaked in the
spring of 1921 when Harding convened the incoming 67th
Congress to write a new tariff. Manila Americans were
thrilled when Congressman Horace Towner of Iowa, the
chairman of the Committee on Insular Affairs who had visited
the colony the previous summer, introduced a joint

resolution opening the prospect of territorial government
for the Philippines.[31] Despite the leadership of their
chairman, however, the members of the committee did not
bother to report the measure, which deflated the soaring
hopes of the American community.

Disappointed when Congress failed to take up the Towner
resolution, the American business community found
consolation in the Fordney-McCumber tariff of 1922.[32] The
postwar slump in commodity prices punctured the wartime
prosperity enjoyed by rural America, and, under pressure to
"do something for the farmer," the Republicans turned to
their favorite nostrum, higher tariffs. The colony had
benefited fortuitously when the Democrats removed the quotas
on Philippine exports in writing the Underwood-Simmons
tariff in 1913. Nine years later the colony received a
comparable windfall when the Fordney-McCumber tariff
established protective duties on vegetable oils, desiccated
coconut, and canned pineapple. Within a few years, American
enterprise and capital were prominent in coconut-oil
production and dominated new industries producing desiccated
coconut and canned pineapple. Philippine exports of coconut
oil and desiccated coconut quickly captured the American
market for these products and exports of canned pineapple to
the United States grew steadily. The Fordney-McCumber
tariff proved a mixed blessing for Manila Americans,
however, as rapid growth in shipments of Philippine coconut
oil alarmed American dairy and vegetable oil interests who
petitioned Congress for quotas on insular shipments of
coconut oil. Frustrated in their efforts to escape
Philippine competition, these interests were driven into the
American independence movement as it gathered strength in
the 1920s.

The interest of Manila Americans in territorial status
remained intense during the visit to the Philippines in 1921
of General Leonard Wood, the presidential candidate of the

19

progressive wing of the Republican Party in 1920, and former
Governor General Forbes, who comprised Harding's "special
investigating mission." Wood and Forbes carefully sounded
opinion across the American community and solicited exhibits
and testimony which afforded Americans ample opportunity to
deprecate the capacity of Filipinos for self-government and
to make known their support for territorial status. As the
mission's stay in the islands drew to a close, the American
Chamber of Commerce met to endorse a resolution that the
colony be converted to the "Territory of Malaya" and given a
territorial government.[33]

Manila Americans were also encouraged to anticipate a
new phase of colonial government when Washington announced
that Wood would be the new governor general. Wood and
Forbes provided few hints as to the government
recommendation they would make, however, which added to the
anxiety with which the American community awaited the
mission's report. With Wood due to return to Manila to take
up his new duties in October 1921, the chamber members
decided to step up pressure for territorial status. To do
so they greeted Wood with a cable, widely circulated to
trade associations and chambers of commerce in the States,
advising against further American investment in the
Philippines until the colony's status was fixed as a
territory. Wood was furious with the action of the chamber
and when the report of the Wood-Forbes Mission appeared,
recommending that the colony continue to be governed under
the Jones Law, the American business community cooled toward
the new governor general.[34]

In December 1921 the Four-Power Pacific Treaty,
committing the United States, Great Britain, Japan, and
France to maintain the military and naval status quo in the
Western Pacific, was signed in Washington. The treaty
prompted widespread speculation that Congress, assured by
the treaty that independence granted the Philippines would

be respected by the signatory powers, would take up the
"Philippine question." A few months later, the Nacionalista
Party leaders Sergio Osmeña and Manuel Quezon led a
"parliamentary mission" to the States, which renewed
speculation in the colony that something was afoot on the
"Philippine question." With the action ten thousand miles
away in Washington, the ACC met to endorse a third
resolution petitioning Congress for territorial status.[35]

   The American elections in 1922 increased substantially
the congressional contingents of Democrats and "progressive"
Republicans who favored independence, and the concern of
Manila Americans for Congress's intentions toward the colony
refused to subside. By the summer of 1923, Governor General
Wood was moving to recover executive powers that had been
vested in his office by the Jones Law but shared with
Filipino leaders by his predecessor. Quezon, who had
wrested the Nacionalista Party leadership from Osmeña,
decided to oppose Wood's actions. This confrontation
exploded spectacularly in the "cabinet crisis" of 1923.
Alarmed that Congress might choose to escape responsibility
for the turbulent colony by enacting independence, the ACC
met to approve a fourth petition for territorial status.[36]

   Although the composition of the incoming 64th Congress
threatened action on the "Philippine question," the American
business community remained complacent during the initial
weeks of the session. In early March the chamber met to
approve a fifth resolution favoring a territorial form of
government "similar to that of Hawaii." The directors of
the chamber also authorized wide distribution in the States
of a pamphlet reminding Americans that their country was
ruling the Philippines by "right of conquest and by
purchase" and asserting that "a form of territorial
government has been established." Meanwhile, both House and
Senate Philippine committees held hearings on early
independence measures which revealed strong sentiment in

Congress for freeing the colony. At the conclusion of the
hearings, Secretary of War John W. Weeks cabled Wood in
Manila that substantial majorities of both houses favored
independence.[37]

Confronted by this alarming development, the American
Chamber of Commerce abandoned its territorial-status crusade
for an alternative strategy. In doing so the chamber
members decided that, although the Constitution empowered
Congress to make all "needful rules" for administering
"territory" acquired by the United States, this authority
did not include the power to alienate American sovereignty.
The chamber contended that an amendment to the Constitution
was required to vest such authority in Congress. Having
satisfied themselves that Congress did not have the power to
free the colony, the chamber members petitioned Congress to
create the "Federated Philippine Islands States" of Luzon,
Visayas, and Mindanao. The chamber also delegated three of
its leading members to go to Washington to oppose any
independence measures.[38] Meanwhile, Republican regulars on
the House committee were able to deflect the drive for early
independence by coalescing behind the Fairfield bill,
drafted by the Bureau of Insular Affairs, which would move
the colony to a new stage of autonomous Filipino government
under residual American sovereignty. However, the Fairfield
bill did not come to a vote as Congress rushed to adjourn
for the nominating conventions of 1924.

The chamber's campaign to deflect congressional
sentiment for independence by questioning the power of
Congress to alienate American sovereignty was no more
effective than its territorial-status crusade. A year and a
half later the chamber invited Congress to surrender its
jurisdiction over the fate of the colonial enterprise by
submitting the "Philippine question" to the American people
in a referendum.[39] Diverse proposals calling upon Congress
to relinquish or share its constitutional power to dispose

of the colony were raised from time to time during the
period of American rule, but they all foundered on
congressional indifference.

The next threat faced by American business in the
colony was the campaign of American sugar, dairy, and
vegetable oil interests for quotas limiting insular
shipments of sugar and coconut oil to the United States.
This issue surfaced in 1928 when Congressman Charles
Timberlake (Colo.) submitted a resolution limiting imports
of Philippine sugar to 500,000 tons. The ACC responded by
joining with the insular government and the Nacionalista
Party in a common front behind the position that so long as
the colony remained under the American flag it would be
"immoral" to restrict insular exports to the United
States.[40]

The concern of the American business community over the
threat of quotas limiting insular exports to the United
States was short-lived. President Hoover convened the new
Congress in 1929 to revise the tariff. In debate on the
sugar schedule, Senator Edwin Broussard (La.) proposed an
amendment limiting shipments of insular sugar to the United
States to 600,000 tons. Debate on Broussard's amendment
revealed strong sentiment for freeing the colony and Senator
William King (Utah), who introduced independence measures in
every Congress following his election to the Senate in 1922,
proposed an amendment converting Broussard's amendment to an
early-independence measure. The Senate rejected the King
amendment by a relatively narrow vote which confirmed the
strength of independence sentiment in Congress. This
incident projected the "Philippine question" to center stage
where it remained until independence legislation
materialized three years later.[41]

The American Chamber of Commerce never deviated in its
opposition to independence and to curtailment of the
colony's trade preference. As independence approached, the

23

American business community found itself powerless to
influence events as Congress drafted independence
legislation and scheduled the gradual elimination of mutual
free trade, which Congress considered a denial of meaningful
Philippine independence.

The American elections of 1930 sharply increased the
Democratic contingents in both Houses and the Philippine
committees scheduled hearings on independence measures when
the new Congress convened in December 1931. The American
Chamber of Commerce confined its lobbying efforts to
resolutions opposing both the Hare and Hawes-Cutting bills
on the ground that the trade provisions of these measures
were "framed to destroy the economic structure of the
Philippine Islands."[42] With this feeble contribution, the
American business community in the Philippines joined the
insular government and the War Department in Washington in
relying upon Hoover's veto to turn back the threat of
independence. Hoover did veto the Hare-Hawes-Cutting law,
but his veto was quickly overridden by substantial margins
in both Houses.

However, independence did not come via the Hare-Hawes-
Cutting law. Quezon was disgruntled by the economic terms
of independence and apprehensive that their success in
obtaining independence legislation might enable Osmeña and/
or Manuel Roxas, who served as the independence mission to
Washington, to challenge successfully his monopoly of
political power. In the end, he decided to try to
precipitate a bargaining confrontation with the incoming
Roosevelt administration in which he would seek terms of
independence more to his liking. To do so, he led a
successful campaign to obtain rejection of the independence
law by the insular legislature.

Quezon's decision to oppose acceptance of the
independence law was welcome to Manila Americans generally,
and from the sidelines of the bitter intra-Nacionalista

24

Party struggle they cheered on the "Anti" faction, led by Quezon, which soundly trounced the "Pro" faction of Osmeña and Roxas. We can be confident that members of the chamber were delighted to find themselves on the winning side for a change. Their glee promptly gave way to chagrin, however, as Quezon's efforts to reopen the economic provisions of the independence law foundered on the indifference of the Roosevelt administration and he was forced to accept Congress's terms of independence, with minor cosmetic changes, in the Tydings-McDuffie Act of 1934.

Within a few weeks of the unanimous decision of the insular legislature to accept the Tydings-McDuffie law, Quezon collaborated with Governor General Frank Murphy and his economic staff in launching a "reciprocity" campaign to reopen the economic terms of independence. Heartened by this development, the ACC joined with its Filipino counterparts, the Chamber of Commerce of the Philippines, the Confederation of Associations of Sugar Planters, the Manila Chamber of Commerce, the Philippine Sugar Association, and other organizations of export producers, to form the Philippine-American Trade Association to support the crusade to preserve the colony's trade preference.[43]

The insular government and the Philippine Legislature drafted legislation to reserve a larger share of the insular market to American manufactures and thereby maintain a more balanced or "reciprocal" trade between the Philippines and the United States. Meanwhile, Quezon junketed to Washington to drum up congressional support for "reciprocity." The Roosevelt administration was more interested in independence than in continuing the colony's dependence on the American market, however, and the "reciprocity" campaign quickly expired.[44]

Quezon was not one to take "no" for an answer, however, and he continued to resist the loss of preferential trade. In the end, he had no choice but to agree to the appointment

by President Roosevelt of the Joint Preparatory Committee on
Philippine Affairs (JPC) to plan the postindependence
transition to nonpreferential trade. To allow the affected
economic interests their day in court, the JPC held hearings
in the United States and in the Philippines during the
summer of 1937. In anticipation of the hearings in Manila,
the Philippine-American Trade Association was revived and
adopted a statement of "Fundamentals" which declared that
"the imposition of import duties by the United States and
the Philippine Islands . . . will be disastrous to the
producers and manufacturers of both countries" and concluded
that "free-trade relations between the two countries should
be continued indefinitely."[45]

American and Philippine interests were out in force for
the hearings both in the United States and in Manila.
Virtually all briefs submitted by economic interests in the
colony--American and Filipino alike--were prefaced by the
statement of "Fundamentals." The president and the counsel
of the American Chamber of Commerce testified at length on
the need for preferential trade, and the president of the
Pacific Commercial Company, the largest American commercial
firm in the islands and long active in the chamber,
represented the Philippine-American Trade Association before
the committee.[46]

When the JPC returned to Washington to plan the
transition to duty-free trade, this task proved
controversial, but ultimately agreement was reached to
recommend a twenty-year transition, beginning in 1941 and
extending through 1960, over which trade preferences would
be dismantled. A bill to carry out the trade transition
reached Congress in 1939, but it encountered rough sledding
as Europe was girding for war, Japan was extending her
control over China, and Congress was uninterested in
extending any aspect of the colonial relationship beyond the
proclamation of independence in 1946. Congress made minor

26

amendments in the economic provisions of the independence
law covering the remaining period of the autonomous
Philippine Commonwealth, which would give way to the
independent Philippine Republic, and postponed decision on
the postindependence phase of the transition to
nonpreferential trade.

War interrupted the Commonwealth phase of the trade
transition at the end of its first year. The war also saw
the internment of Manila Americans, extensive economic
dislocation as Japan's prospects dwindled, and widespread
destruction during the liberation. The island economy was
prostrate at the war's end and Americans in the Philippines
were fully occupied by the tasks they faced in resuming a
more normal peacetime life. The American Chamber of
Commerce was reactivated within a month of the return of the
American army to Manila, and the *American Chamber of
Commerce Journal* resumed publication in December 1945.

With independence imminent, Congress turned to the task
of tying off the loose ends of four decades of colonial rule
and four years of war. Two major but interrelated tasks
faced Congress: American participation in rehabilitation of
war damage in the colony and scheduling the dismantling of
preferential trade. Extensive hearings were held by the
Ways and Means Committee, but they were dominated by
officials of the executive branch, representatives of the
Commonwealth government, and members of Congress. There was
negligible input into the hearings from Americans with
business interests in the Philippines.

The activities ten thousand miles away in Washington
did not go unnoticed by the reactivated ACC in Manila. When
former U.S. High Commissioner Paul McNutt attempted to
revive his proposal for a "realistic re-examination" of
independence in March 1945, the directors of the chamber
approved a statement affirming that the ACC would not be
concerned with "political questions." A year later, with

independence scheduled to be proclaimed on July 4, the July issue of the *American Chamber of Commerce Journal* included an editorial critical of the "invidious" parity provision of the recently enacted Bell Trade Act requiring Filipinos to amend their constitution to extend national treatment to Americans and their enterprises in the exploitation of natural resources and the operation of public utilities. The editorial did not meet the approval of all chamber members, however, and the February 1947 issue of the *Journal* included an insert signed by the president of the ACC stating that the editorial "merely represented the individual view of the author." It concluded, "The position of the American Chamber of Commerce is that the parity question is one for the decision of the Filipino people" and committed the chamber to "take no part in the controversy." Within a few months, the *Journal* had a new editor.[47]

The Philippine Rehabilitation Act of 1946 assured Filipinos and their new republic substantial amounts of American assistance as they faced the task of repairing the ravages of war. In writing the companion Bell Trade Act, Congress proposed to revive the prostrate Philippine economy by continuing mutual free trade for eight years, followed by twenty years over which mutual trade-preferences would be gradually dismantled. This transition was completed in mid-1974.

IV

The track record of the American business community, as it was organized to focus and amplify the voice of that community behind efforts to influence colonial policy, strongly suggests that as lobbyists these American businessmen were "born losers." They spoke with one voice as they advocated immigration of coolie labor, the extension of coastwise shipping policy to the colony, a panoply of incentives to induce development by American enterprise and

capital, indefinite retention of the colony, territorial
status, and continuation of preferential trade, and as they
opposed quantitative restrictions on Philippine exports to
the United States. Thanks to Taft, they were on the winning
side when mutual free trade was initiated in 1909, but there
is scant evidence that their support was a significant
factor in establishing this policy. In the 1920s and 1930s,
they found themselves allied with virtually every segment of
population in the colony--Filipino and American--in efforts
to prolong preferential trade as the independence movement
in the States gathered strength. My reading of the history
of that period supports the conclusion that in writing
independence legislation in 1932, and in drafting the Bell
Trade Act in 1946, Congress insisted that preferential trade
be dismantled with "all deliberate speed."

The business community of Manila Americans had plenty
of company. The American community as a whole spoke with
one voice and what it had to say was predictable. There was
no significant body of Americans in the Philippines that did
not support indefinite retention in some form or other and
preferential trade. An occasional American deviant would
speak up for independence, but to do so courted peer
pressure approaching ostracism.

The ineffectiveness of Manila Americans as they sought
to mold colonial policy to their liking is not hard to
understand. Their proprietary interest in the colony was
felt intensely, but they did not comprise a microcosm of the
larger American community; they marched to a different
drummer. For an overwhelming proportion of Americans the
"Philippine question" had ceased to be a significant issue
in domestic politics by the time the business community of
Manila Americans formed the American Chamber of Commerce in
1920. Americans generally were agreed that their government
should bestow independence on the colony and that
independence should have an economic as well as a political

dimension. Americans generally did not question the power
of Congress to determine the specific nature of these
dimensions of independence; they took for granted that this
was an aspect of United States sovereignty over the island
colony. Moreover, the Democratic Party, which opposed the
imperial venture from the start and proclaimed America's
purpose to grant independence to the colony in the Jones
Law, was gathering strength and was determined to shed the
Philippine incubus when the party's congressional contingent
reached sufficient size to do so. Under these circumstances
the campaign of Manila Americans--who comprised less than
one ten-thousandth of the American population--to deflect
the will of the wider American society was doomed to
futility.

Notes

1. Henry F. Pringle, *The Life and Times of William Howard
    Taft*, 2 vols. (New York: Farrar & Rinehart, 1939),
    1:160-62.

2. U.S. Congress, House, *Messages of the
    President . . . December 3, 1900*, H. Doc. 1, 56th
    Cong., 2d sess., 1900, 34-40.

3. U.S. Congress, Senate, *Report of the Philippine
    Commission to the Secretary of War, November 30, 1900*,
    S. Doc. 112, 56th Cong., 2d sess., 1900, 32.

4. For a brief survey of the organization of business
    interests in the islands in the early years of American
    rule, see W. Cameron Forbes, *The Philippine Islands*,
    2 vols. (Boston: Houghton-Mifflin Co., 1928), 2:183-86.

5. U.S. Constitution, art. IV, sec. 3; U.S. Congress, S.
    bill 2355, 11 Jan. 1900, 56th Cong., 2d sess., 1900.

6. *Report of the Philippine Commission . . . November 30,
    1900*, 7, 34.

7. Taft to Root, 2 Jan. 1900, ibid., 5-6.

8. U.S. Public Law (PL) 803, 2 Mar. 1901, 31 Stat. 910.

9. Root to Taft, 5 Mar. 1901, U.S. National Archives, Bureau of Insular Affairs, Record Group 350, 141-44½ (hereafter cited as BIA, plus file number).

10. U.S. Philippine Commission, 1900-1916, *Report of the Philippine Commission to the Secretary of War . . . 1901*, 4 vols. (Washington, D.C.: Government Printing Office, 1901), 1:148-50 (hereafter cited as *RPC 1901*).

11. U.S. PL 28, 8 Mar. 1902, 32 Stat. 54; U.S. PL 235, 1 July 1902, 32 Stat. 691.

12. Speech given at Montpelier, Vermont, 26 Aug. 1904, BIA, 3862-75. See also U.S. Congress, House, *Duties on Philippine Products, Hearings before the House Committee on Ways and Means on H.R. 17752*, 58th Cong., 3d sess., 1905, 84; and U.S. Congress, House, *The Duty of Americans in the Philippines*, H. Doc. 191, 58th Cong., 2d sess., 1904, 8.

13. U.S. PL 5, 5 Aug. 1909, 36 Stat. 11, par. 5. For background on the "gentleman's agreement," see Clarence R. Edwards to Governor General James F. Smith, 10 Apr. 1909, and memorandum, Frank McIntyre for Edwards, 14 July 1909, BIA, C1250-83, 125; Carman N. Smith to Taft, 24 Nov. 1908, BIA, C1242-62.

14. Philippine Islands (P.I.), Bureau of the Census, *Census of the Philippine Islands . . . 1903*, 4 vols. (Manila: Bureau of Printing, 1905), 4:565-74; P.I., Bureau of Customs, *Annual Report of the Collector of Customs, 1940* (Manila: Bureau of Printing, 1941), table 2, p. 84.

15. American Chamber of Commerce (ACC), Manila, to McKinley, 19 Dec. 1901; P. Krafft, report for Brewster

Cameron, undated; Barry Baldwin to the Secretary of War, 28 Feb. 1902; Wright to Taft, 1 Mar. 1902; all in BIA, C1246-8, 43, 15, 16.

16. U.S. Congress, Senate Committee on the Philippines, *Affairs in the Philippine Islands*, S. Doc. 331, 3 vols., 57th Cong., 1st sess., 1902, 1:846-48.

17. "Statement Showing Estimate of American Capital Investment in the Philippine Islands," 5 Aug. 1911, BIA, 23908-1.

18. Forbes Journal, vol. 1, 2 Nov. 1904, W. Cameron Forbes Papers, Houghton Library, Harvard University.

19. *Duties on Philippine Products, Hearings . . . on H.R. 17752*, 84; U.S. Congress, House, *Philippine Tariff, Hearings before the Committee on Ways and Means on H.R. 3*, 59th Cong., 1st sess., 1906; U.S. Congress, House, *Tariff Hearings, Hearings before the Committee on Ways and Means*, H. Doc. 1505, 60th Cong., 2d sess., 1909; P.I., *Hearings before the Secretary of War and the Congressional Party, Aug. 29-30, 1905* (Manila: Bureau of Printing, 1905).

20. The activities of the Manila Merchants Association, beginning in 1908, are chronicled in BIA, 17607-0, 1, 10, 14, 28, 29.

21. U.S. PL 16, 3 Oct. 1913, 38 Stat. 114, sec. 4, par. C.

22. Republican National Committee, *Republican Campaign Textbook, 1912* (Philadelphia: Dunlap Printing Co., 1912), 284-85.

23. U.S. Congress, House, H. bill 22143, 62d Cong., 2d sess., 1911; Forbes, *Philippine Islands*, 2:208.

24. U.S. Congress, House, H. bill 18459, 63d Cong., 2d sess., 1914.

25. U.S. Congress, Senate, *Government of the Philippine Islands, Hearings before the Senate Committee on the Philippines on H.R. 18459*, 63d Cong., 3d sess., 1915.

26. U.S. Congress, Senate, S. bill 381, 64th Cong., 1st sess., 1916; *Congressional Record*, 64th Cong., 1st sess., 1916, 1250.

27. Kinkaid to McIntyre, 23 Dec. 1915, BIA, 4325-186; "Resolutions Adopted by the Manila Merchants Association, 25 Dec. 1916," BIA, 4325-228A.

28. U.S. War Department, Bureau of Insular Affairs, *Annual Report of the Governor General of the Philippine Islands, 1920* (Washington, D.C.: Government Printing Office, 1920), 69; George F. Luthringer, *The Gold Exchange Standard of the Philippines* (Princeton: Princeton University Press, 1934), app. E, p. 274.

29. *Congressional Record*, 7 Dec. 1920, 66th Cong., 3d sess., 1920, 33; *New York Times*, 8 Dec. 1920, p. 1.

30. *Editorials and Letters From the Open Forum Appearing in the Manila Times During August and September 1920, Relative to a Territorial Form of Government* (Manila: n.p., 1920); George H. Fairchild to Harding, 11 Apr. 1921, BIA, 364-99.

31. U.S. Congress, House, *House Joint Resolution 68*, 21 Apr. 1921, 67th Cong., 1st sess., 1921; *Manila Times*, 25 Apr. 1921, and *Philippines Herald*, 24 Apr. 1921, BIA, 364-423A, 423B.

32. U.S. PL 318, 21 Sept. 1922, 42 Stat. 858, sec. 301.

33. *New York Times*, 13 Sept. 1921, p. 16.

34. *New York Times*, 15 Oct. 1921, p. 16, and 24 Oct. 1921, p. 26; U.S. Congress, House, *Conditions in the Philippine Islands, Report of the Special Mission to the Philippine Islands to the Secretary of War, 8 Oct. 1921*, H. Doc. 235, 67th Cong., 2d sess., 1922.

35. *New York Times*, 27 May 1922, p. 12.

36. *New York Times*, 16 Nov. 1923, p. 19.

37. Norbert Lyons, *The Philippine Problem Presented from a New Angle* (Manila: n.p., 1924), 6-8; *New York Times*, 15 Mar. 1924, p. 7; Heath (President, ACC) to the Secretary of War, 21 Feb. 1924, in U.S. Congress, Senate, *Philippine Independence, Hearings before the Committee on Territories and Insular Possessions on S. 912*, 68th Cong., 1st sess., 1924, 61; McIntyre to Wood, 1 Mar. 1924, BIA, 4325-after 287; McIntyre to Wood, 1 Mar. 1924, BIA, 364-after 499.

38. *New York Times*, 11 Apr. 1924, p. 15; Wood to the Secretary of War, 7 May 1924, BIA, 4325-310.

39. *New York Times*, 29 Nov. 1925, p. 29.

40. U.S. Congress, House, *House Joint Resolution 214*, 23 Feb. 1928, 70th Cong., 1st sess., 1928; ACC to the Secretary of War, 7 Mar. 1929, BIA, C1246-164.

41. U.S. PL 361, 17 June 1930, 46 Stat. 590, sec. 301. For debates on the Broussard and King amendments, see *Congressional Record*, 9 Oct. 1929, 71st Cong., 1st sess., 1929, 4062-71, 4369-99.

42. *New York Times*, 2 Apr. 1932, p. 23; 21 June 1933, p. 37; and 24 Jan. 1934, p. 12.

43. Philippine-American Trade Association, *Program of the Reciprocity Movement* (reprinted from *Sugar News*, 16 Sept. 1935), copy in Frank Murphy Papers, box 54, file 54-10, Michigan Historical Collections, Ann Arbor; *New York Times*, 18 July 1934, p. 10; C. K. Moser, U.S. Department of Commerce, memorandum, "Recent Developments Relating to the Philippine Islands," 31 Aug. 1934, BIA, C1246-181.

44. Murphy to Cox, 9 Aug. 1934, Frank Murphy Papers, box
    51, file 51-45; *Congressional Record*, 74th Cong., 1st
    sess., 1934, 7541; *New York Times*, 27 Oct. 1934, p. 9.

45. U.S. Department of State, *Report of the Joint
    Preparatory Committee on Philippine Affairs, May 20,
    1938*, 4 vols. (Washington, D.C.: Government Printing
    Office, 1938). For statement of "Fundamentals," see
    ibid., vol. 3, group 1, p. 2.

46. Ibid., 2:572-603.

47. Lewis E. Gleeck, Jr., *The Manila Americans (1901-1964)*
    (Manila: Carmelo & Bauermann, 1977), 274-75; *American
    Chamber of Commerce Journal*, July 1946 and February
    1947. The offending editorial is reprinted in Shirley
    Jenkins, *American Economic Policy Toward the
    Philippines* (Stanford: Stanford University Press,
    1954), 80.

AMERICA'S "PERMISSIVE" COLONIALISM:
JAPANESE BUSINESS IN THE PHILIPPINES, 1899-1941

Grant K. Goodman

No matter what may happen in the world, the
traditional friendship between Japan and the
Philippines should not be disturbed.

Kimura Atsushi
Former Consul General of Japan
in the Philippines
September 10, 1941

For over a decade my research interest, as a historian
of Japan, has focused on the relationship between Japan and
South and Southeast Asia during the period from
approximately the Russo-Japanese War through the Pacific
War. In that context I have given particular attention to
Japanese-Philippine relations and to Japanese-Indian
relations. While comparisons are not always useful, certain
generalizations nevertheless have emerged in the course of
these studies.

Both in colonial India and in the colonial Philippines
the concern of the Japanese government and of the Japanese
business community, working then as now in close concert,
was almost exclusively economic. While the Philippines had
a significant immigrant Japanese population, about thirty
thousand in December 1941, India had almost none. In Japan
prior to World War II, knowledge of both colonies was
minimal and serious interest in these two "fellow" Asian

entities was almost nonexistent. In fact, what information there was consisted overwhelmingly of Japanese translations of British and American books. Complementarily, knowledge of Japan in India and the Philippines in the prewar era derived almost entirely from British and American sources and opinions. For both India and the Philippines, an examination of the archives of the Ministry of Foreign Affairs in Tokyo reveals that Japanese diplomats in the two colonies were astute, informed, and tough observers who reported trenchantly and in great detail, thus providing an impressively reliable picture of conditions in their assigned bailiwicks.

During the colonial period in both Delhi and Manila there were varying degrees of unease about Japanese intentions toward India and the Philippines. The British raj, at times seeming almost desperate to reinforce its hold on the subcontinent, evidenced a fair degree of paranoia about the presumed multiple dangers posed by Japan to India. Such fears persisted despite the almost total lack of evidence of any serious Japanese threat to Indian security. In the Philippine case, for the most part, the Americans seemed to make a concerted effort to minimize any danger to the islands from Japan, even though the possibility of aggressive action by Japanese forces seemed to be on the increase as American colonial rule neared an end. In fact, the American colonial authorities in the Philippines were as convinced as the Filipino political leaders that viable independence for the colony was greatly dependent upon the good will of the Japanese empire.

Moreover, since the concept of "permissive" colonialism, as used in this paper, is based on the contention that from the outset of its colonial rule in the Philippines the United States was a reluctant colonial mentor, interference in economic activities such as those of the Japanese, which would seemingly ultimately advance the

economic well-being of the Philippines, was minimized.
Indeed, as an "uncolonial" colonial power, the United States
never had a trained colonial civil service committed to
"defending" American interests in the Philippines.
Moreover, psychologically burdened with guilt about colonial
control of the Philippines and repeatedly articulating the
rhetoric of the goal of training the Filipinos for self-
government, the Americans became increasingly dependent upon
and manipulated by a very skillful indigenous elite. While
members of this dominant social-economic-political Filipino
clique utilized nationalist slogans to gain public favor for
themselves and foster public fervor for independence, behind
the scenes they developed close and useful ties with their
reticent colonial masters who, then as now, much preferred
American-style constitutional politics to the complexities
of economics. As David Sturtevant has written, the
Americans, by virtue of their emphasis on "political
fundamentalism," "strengthened the social legacy of Spain:
elitists derived augmented powers; peasants inherited
mounting squalor."[1]

Further, in economic terms American interests in the
Philippines were never of great importance. No significant
number of Americans ever settled in the islands. While some
few American corporations developed sizable investments in
the Philippines, for example, Dole Pineapple and Benguet
Consolidated Mining, the overall stake of American capital
there remained relatively small. In fact, as both the
Japanese and the Filipinos well understood, it was largely
pressure from domestic American economic interests in a
severe depression era--sugar beet growers, rope
manufacturers, and the like--that influenced Congress to
pass the Tydings-McDuffie Act of 1934. This legislation
promised the Philippines full independence in 1946, after a
ten-year transition period of Commonwealth status during
which a United States High Commissioner, representing the

American president, would continue to control foreign affairs and defense.

Here again the Japanese were acute observers of both the American and Philippine scenes since they, unlike many other foreign observers, firmly believed after passage of the independence law (and, in fact, much earlier) that the United States would indeed pull out of the islands. As the information provided below will suggest, while the Americans continued to exercise sovereignty over the Philippines, the Japanese moved vigorously and purposefully to fill what they saw to be a potential economic void, one which they felt certain the Filipinos themselves could not fill. Finally, it also should be emphasized that, during the 1930s in particular, United States officials in the Philippines, reflecting policies determined in Washington, were extremely reluctant to encourage actions which would unnecessarily antagonize the Japanese government and further exacerbate the already difficult relations between America and Japan.

Japanese trade with, and investment in, the Philippines began in the nineteenth century under the Spaniards. In 1888 the first Japanese consul was appointed to the Philippines. He brought with him over 140 different articles to exhibit in order to encourage and develop trade: silk, crepe, cotton handkerchiefs, porcelain, glass, toilet soaps, and so on.[2] In 1898 the first Japanese-owned retail store in Manila opened and offered, in addition to a complete line of dry goods, such typically Japanese items as lacquerware and Satsuma chinaware. In 1901 the firm, Mitsui Bussan Kaisha, opened a branch on the second floor of the "Nippon Bazar," the name given to the aforementioned retail outlet. By 1914 there were 20 Japanese-owned firms and commercial establishments operating in the Philippines. By 1920 there were 40 and by 1934 there were 200, of which 139 were locally organized and 61 were branches of Japan-based concerns.[3]

Statistically, the increasing importance of Japan in
Philippine trade can be easily demonstrated by the following
figures: in 1899 Japan was the fifth-largest trading partner
of the Philippines with a total trade value of 2.5 million
pesos; in 1909 Japan had dropped to tenth-largest, but the
value of Japan-Philippines trade had risen to 3.5 million
pesos; in 1919 Japan was number three, with a total value of
42.1 million pesos; and in 1929 Japan was, as Japan was to
remain until the Pacific War, number two, although, because
of the world depression, the actual value of the trade had
declined slightly to 38.1 million pesos.[4] In 1937 an all-
time high was reached in prewar Philippine-Japanese trade,
when the total value amounted to more than 52 million pesos,
10 percent of the Commonwealth's foreign trade.[5]

Prior to 1905, Japan-Philippines trade had been fairly
evenly balanced between imports and exports, but from 1906
to 1911 the trade pattern favored Japan. Between 1912 and
1918, exports and imports between the two countries were
again mutually in balance, but after 1918 the Philippines
was faced with a continuous and growing trade imbalance due
to an excess of imports from Japan. This situation was
characterized by a progressive expansion on the part of
Japan of the number and variety of items, as well as of the
quantity of individual items offered for export. Quite the
opposite was true in the Philippine case where, although the
actual number of exportable items increased very slightly,
the nature of the "new" goods was economically insignificant
and the actual amounts involved were minimal. By 1938 the
Sino-Japanese War and Japan's extensive economic controls
began to affect Japan-Philippines trade. Japan's exports to
the Philippines fell off considerably, but Japan's purchases
of Philippine raw materials increased (especially metals,
hemp, and lumber) so that in 1939 and 1940 the trade balance
was reversed.

The principal exports of the Philippines to Japan were abaca fiber, lumber, leaf tobacco, kapok, copra, coconut oil, and gums and resins. From Japan the Philippines imported textiles, coal and coke, glassware, matches, paper and paper articles, iron and steel, and fish and fish products. While Japanese investments in the Philippines were relatively small before 1932, key areas of the Philippine economy were attracting Japanese capital. For, despite a certain amount of either ineffective or unenforced restrictive legislation, Japanese real-estate holdings included valuable residential and business properties in the major urban centers, timber lands, mineral lands, and agricultural lands. Japanese shipping was also moving into a position of dominance in the Philippine carrying trade. Other enterprises in which Japanese investors played a significant role were gravel and crushed rock companies, the printing and binding industry, and the manufacture of bricks and tiles, boxes and bags, ice cream, shoes, confectionaries, and beer.[6]

The Japanese had also moved successfully with energy and capital into the Philippine fishing industry. Certainly, given the fish-consuming dietary habits of the Filipinos and the natural wealth in fish of the waters surrounding the islands, one might have expected highly developed techniques of fish catching and therefore a cheap and plentiful supply of fish. Unfortunately, such was not the case. Lacking technical skill, capital, and initiative, Filipino fishermen had advanced little since pre-Spanish days. Deep-sea fishing was practically unknown, and inshore fishing was limited, too, by inadequate and inefficient methods. The tropical Philippine climate, marked by continuous high temperatures and humidity, also discouraged improvements because of the rapid decay of fish after the catch. Some commentators have also criticized both the Spanish and American colonial administrations for failing to encourage the improvement of Philippine fishing techniques and skills.

By 1930 Japanese domination of the Philippine fishing industry was a fact. Four hundred Japanese fishermen were operating sixty-four power fishing boats in Manila Bay and thirty-six more deep-sea power vessels in the Gulf of Davao, an investment of half a million pesos. The Japanese had brought to the Philippines such innovations as swift, powered, fishing vessels, the beam trawl, and the trap net, as well as scientific survey-ships which pinpointed from year to year the richest fishing grounds. Moreover, many of the Japanese engaged in fishing in the Philippines were graduates of Japanese fishery schools. If one adds to these advantages the same industriousness and emphasis on organization which the Japanese brought to their other activities, the Japanese success story is easily understood.

Not until 1930, when an estimated 80 percent of the fish products brought to the Manila market were supplied by the Japanese,[7] did the Philippine government attempt to curb Japanese fishing activities. In that year the insular legislature passed restrictive legislation which was vetoed by Governor General Dwight Davis (after receiving a strong letter of protest from the Japanese consul general) on grounds that the bill was carelessly drawn. However, in December 1932 the so-called Fisheries Act was approved by Governor General Theodore Roosevelt, Jr., coincidentally the most anti-Japanese of the American chief executives in the Philippines. This law provided for a control procedure by which all commercial fishing vessels of more than three tons in operation at the time of the promulgation of the law would be licensed, but subsequently aliens could only engage in fishing by participation in corporations in which "at least sixty-one percent of the capital stock belongs wholly to citizens of the Philippine Islands or of the United States."[8]

43

That this law never proved effective and that Japanese domination of fishing continued up to the outbreak of war is not surprising. At the time of the passage of the Fisheries Act, a significant segment of informed opinion felt that such discriminatory legislation would only retard Philippine economic development and would remove an important stimulus to Filipino fishermen. Further, it was believed by many that the Philippine government might well lose a potentially important source of tax revenue and that Filipino laborers might be deprived of a fairly lucrative area of employment. This law also created new problems, such as poaching by unauthorized Japanese fishermen, and, most importantly, the so-called dummy system by which fishing boats were simply registered in the name of a Filipino who was paid a certain number of pesos each month for the use of his name while Japanese continued to operate the boats. Since, unfortunately, there were often close ties between Filipino politicians and dummy owners, investigations and exposes of this situation never seemed to achieve results. In fact, some observers went so far as to suggest that the most significant impetus to the passage of the Fisheries Act was the hope of some Philippine politicos and lawyers to profit from it as dummies rather than the publicly stated fear that Japanese economic encroachment was a possible forerunner to political penetration. The average annual dummy's fee of 150 pesos was simply assumed by the Japanese to be an unavoidable expense of doing business, the cost of "protection" for a generally very profitable enterprise.

Japanese interest in the potential of Philippine mineral resources dated from at least 1911 when geologists from the firm, Mitsui Bussan, spent some months in the islands studying iron ore deposits and attempting to negotiate certain business arrangements which at that time failed to reach fruition. In 1917 the Kuhara Mining Company of Tokyo began to exploit the Calambayanga site in Camarines Norte, Luzon, but terminated operations the following year

44

because the yield was low and expenses were excessive.
Other Japanese interests purchased considerable quantities
of bituminous limestone mined near Balete on the island of
Leyte.[9] The subsequent development of extraction for export
of such minerals as iron ore, chromium, manganese, copper,
and gold was due in large measure to the growing demands of
the Japanese market and to the stimulus of Japanese capital.
By 1940, base metals made up some 40 percent of the value of
Philippine trade with Japan.[10]

Efforts by Japanese business interests to open up the
great stands of commercial timber in the Philippines also
met with notable success. However, the real extent of
prewar Japanese involvement in lumbering is extremely
difficult to determine, again because of the extensive and
successful use of dummies. Perhaps the leader in this field
was the Philippine Lumber Exportation Company, a subsidiary
of the Nakamura Steamship Company of Kobe, whose president,
Nakamura Seishichiro, a leading businessman and financier,
was a close personal friend of the leading prewar Filipino
political figure, Manuel L. Quezon. The Philippine Lumber
Exportation Company also acted as sole agent in Japan,
Korea, and Manchuria for three other major Philippine timber
enterprises. In addition, the Philippine Lumber Exportation
Company had its own logging station at Casiguran, Tayabas
(later Quezon) Province, the home territory of Quezon. In
1941 Japanese investment in Philippine timber ranked at
least third, behind that of Philippine and American capital,
but it may well have ranked higher because of the concealed
Japanese interest in both Filipino and American firms.

It is especially informative to peruse the extensive
correspondence between Quezon and both Nakamura and Ando
Kinuzo, managing director and general manager of the
Philippine Lumber Exportation Company.[11] The tenor of the
writing is so intimate and so personal that one is struck by
the closeness of these friendships. Moreover, to witness

the kind of ties that existed between leaders of the
Japanese business community in the islands and the highest
echelon of Philippine politics is to gain an insight into
one of the principal bases of the strong bonds between Japan
and the Philippines that developed during the 1930s despite
the gradual deterioration of Japanese-American relations.

Perhaps the single overriding aim of the leaders of the
Japanese community in the Philippines was to try to bring
about among the Philippine leadership a recognition of what
the Japanese insistently described as the "complementarity"
of the two economies. To this end the Japanese assiduously
cultivated the trust and friendship of a variety of key
Filipinos. Not only was this commercial diplomacy at its
best (and a style at which the Japanese excel), but it
created an ease of rapport between Japanese and Filipinos
which resulted concretely in the improvement of Japan's
economic position in the Philippines in an era of political
antagonism between Japan and the United States. In this
regard it should be noted also that the Japanese, far better
than most Americans, understood the intensely personal
nature of Philippine society and consciously operated on a
very personalized basis, working to develop deep personal
attachments in a way that is alien to American society and
in a style for which Americans have no patience.

Despite these intense efforts, Japan's share of
Philippine trade remained proportionately quite limited.
However, it was believed by many Japanese and Filipinos that
the preferential tariff relationship between the United
States and the Philippines was responsible for keeping these
figures so low.[12] Therefore, with the promise of
independence in 1946 and an anticipated diminution of free
trade between the former colonial master and its
independent-to-be offspring, the prospects for Japan seemed
bright indeed. Meanwhile, in a series of somewhat
ambivalent moves, Filipino politicians were on the one hand

trying to pass legislation which would be restrictive toward Japanese trade (and thus prove to the American Congress that independence would not mean the end of the profitable Philippine market for American traders) and on the other hand trying to encourage the expansion by Japan of her trade with the Philippines in anticipation of independence. In the fall of 1932 the Philippine Japanese Merchants Association entered a formal protest against certain tariff bills pending before the Philippine Legislature. The Japanese consul general also expressed the view that the proposed bills were discriminatory and were in violation of the most-favored-nation clause of the United States–Japan commercial treaty of 1911. In particular, he objected to Philippine Senate bill no. 173 which proposed that customs be levied on the basis of par currencies. While this act was presumably directed at all countries with depreciated currencies, Consul General Kimura Atsushi stated that it would impose upon Japanese goods a duty more than double the present rate by arbitrarily fixing the value of yen currency.[13]

In his reply, rejecting the protest and "deeply regretting" their different points of view, Governor General Roosevelt wrote to Kimura:

> I have given your protest against Senate Bill No. 173 most careful consideration and feel that you have misinterpreted its purport. The Bill in its essence is not discriminatory against any nation, for all are treated alike therein. Indeed, it is the reverse of discriminatory, for it provides a method for the standardization of values which prevents inequalities arising between nations because of some temporary fluctuation in exchange in their currencies.[14]

What neither Kimura nor Roosevelt perhaps realized was that
this legislation was really put forward in the Philippine
Legislature to support the efforts of the Osrox Mission
which was in Washington pressuring for Philippine
independence. In short, the Filipino legislators were
saying to their American counterparts that the American
market would be protected even if independence was granted.

Yet, as independence approached, spokesmen for Japan
were becoming more direct in their statements and were
increasingly addressing themselves to their Filipino
audiences and tending to ignore the continued American
presence. For example, Watanabe Kaoru, commercial agent in
the Philippines for the Japanese Ministry of Commerce and
Industry, urged the Filipinos to get ready for independence
by taking a series of concrete steps which he listed as: the
development of diversified foreign markets for Philippine
products, the development of home industries for greater
domestic stability, the development of local agricultural
production so as to eliminate the importation of foreign
foodstuffs, the development of uncultivated lands, the
planting and cultivating of cotton, the building of a canvas
shoe factory, the opening of a moderate-size iron foundry,
and the improvement of fruit-bearing plants.[15] In
retrospect, one must say that this was excellent advice
while also admitting that in every one of these suggested
actions there was an obvious role for either Japanese
capital or Japanese technical skill. Again, Consul General
Kimura, in an address to the Pan Pacific Association of
Manila, called for the production in the Philippines of more
of the raw materials needed in Japan, for closer attention
to reducing the cost of production of such items in the
Philippines so that their products might be more
competitive, for the establishment of a Philippine trade
mission in Japan, and for the adjustment of the monetary
system of the Philippines to the standards of other
countries, an obvious reference to the depreciated Japanese

yen. Kimura further urged the Philippines to raise cotton
and try to gain a share of Japan's 360 million yen worth of
annual cotton imports.[16]

In an address at the University of the Philippines,
Kimura counseled Filipinos not to erect tariff barriers
against Japanese goods. He also advised them to depreciate
the peso to bring it in line with the yen, give up the dream
of future trade relations with the United States, and
seriously consider the development of free trade between
Japan and the Philippines to replace the American free
market, which, he said, would be terminated with
independence. Finally, he sounded a muted warning to
Philippine officialdom when he said, "In dealing with a
matter which may affect future relations with foreign
countries, especially with the Oriental countries, you must
take the utmost care to prevent any possible
misunderstanding."[17] Kimura was most likely directing his
remarks to the members of the legislature who just one month
earlier had received a message from Governor General Frank
Murphy urging them to respond to the generous trade
provisions of the Tydings-McDuffie Act by considering
raising tariffs against Japanese textiles in order to
protect American manufacturers.

That message had undoubtedly been the result of
tremendous pressure brought to bear on Murphy by American
textile exporters, and it is questionable whether Murphy
ever seriously intended to have such a measure passed.
Quezon, too, was inundated by similar communications from
American textile interests. All of this was the result of a
sharp rise in Philippine cotton-textile imports from Japan
in 1933 and 1934.[18] For example, a report issued on
January 15, 1934, showed that the sale of Japanese goods in
the Philippines during 1933 had increased some 50 percent,
while United States sales decreased 12 percent, and that the
principal Japanese gain had been made in the sale of cotton

textiles, in which Japan's share of the market had jumped to over 50 percent.[19] Nevertheless, overall trade figures released in March 1934 showed that 83.2 percent of Philippine trade was still being conducted with the United States as compared to Japan's 4.6 percent share.[20] In fact, the increase in Japan's share of the Philippine textile market during 1933 and 1934 had nothing to do with tariffs. In these years Philippine tariffs, which had never been prohibitively high, were little different from those of preceding years. Rather, Japan's gain in the textile market could be attributed to four other factors: (1) superior merchandising (in a price, not a quality, market), plus long-term credit, centralized distribution, and the latest manufacturing techniques; (2) rising prices of American textiles as a result of National Recovery Administration (NRA) regulations; (3) shipping strikes in the United States that gave the Japanese a chance to penetrate deeply the market in the Philippines; and (4) the end of a boycott of Japanese goods by Chinese merchants in the Philippines.

Pressures ebbed and flowed about members of the Philippine Legislature. Some legislators felt that the decision on the textile tariff question represented, in effect, a choice for the future between Japan and the United States. A "well-organized Japanese-financed" lobby known as the Consumers League was particularly active in urging legislators to be sensitive to the need to keep Philippine living costs as low as possible by maintaining the flow into the islands of inexpensive Japanese goods.[21] Many legislators, however, were seriously concerned lest the failure to pass anti-Japanese economic legislation be considered ingratitude by the American Congress which might then retaliate against the Philippines.

Immediately, the decision of the legislature was to take no decision. Instead, at the request and at the expense of the Philippine Legislature, a special American

congressional committee was invited to visit the islands to
make recommendations about future relationships between the
Philippines and the United States.[22] This action was
undoubtedly not only attributable to the textile problem,
but even more to two sudden blows at the Philippine economy
struck by the American Congress almost directly on the heels
of the Tydings-McDuffie Act.

The Jones-Costigan Sugar Act of 1934 had provided
specific quotas for domestic American sugar producers but
had left the quotas for other areas to be fixed by the
secretary of agriculture. In June, Secretary
Henry A. Wallace set the Philippine quota for 1934,
retroactive to January 1, at just over 1 million short tons,
actually less than the amount of Philippine sugar already
exported to the United States that year. Another half-
million tons would in fact be sent to the United States in
1934, but would be subtracted from the quota for 1935, which
had been set below 1 million tons, leaving a net quota (for
1935) of under 0.5 million tons, less than one-third of the
previous year's production.[23]

Moreover, domestic American producers of fats and oils
lobbied into the Revenue Act of 1934 a provision (section
602½) which levied a processing tax of three cents per pound
on coconut oil, a burden equivalent to 200 percent of the
then-prevailing market price of coconut oil. The word
"processing" was obviously a euphemism since the tax was
nothing more than a toll levied against Philippine producers
for the benefit of American oil interests. Even the
provision that proceeds collected from the tax were to be
returned to the insular treasury did little or nothing to
soften the impact of this restrictive legislation since an
amendment also stated that such payments were to cease at
once if "at any time the Philippine government provides by
law for any subsidy to be paid to the producers of copra,
coconut oil or allied products."[24]

Clearly, a major beneficiary of these harsh measures was Japan. It was the Japanese who had been urging the Philippines to recognize that independence would bring an end to its protected niche in the American market, that a reorientation of its economic life would necessarily take place, and that Japan was the logical successor to America in the Philippine trade pattern. As one *New York Times* correspondent so aptly put it, "The United States is showing the Philippines out, and Japan is leading them in."[25]

A concurrent report to the State Department from Ambassador Joseph C. Grew in Tokyo concerned what seemed to be characteristic Japanese efforts in this direction.[26] Grew recounted in detail the contents of an article which appeared in a special supplement of the *Osaka Mainichi* newspaper. The writer was one Asari Kenji, an official of a textile company, whose views, according to Grew, might be considered typical of his industry. Asari's thesis was that the Philippine sugar industry would collapse after independence because of American tariffs and that Filipinos should immediately begin to plant abandoned sugar lands in cotton; thus, prosperity for "the two oriental races" would result from an exchange of Philippine raw cotton for Japanese manufactured goods. As of 1935, when these ideas were being bruited about by the Japanese, the production of raw cotton in the Philippines was practically nonexistent. However, the Japanese were suggesting that the new restrictions being imposed on Philippine products by the United States would inevitably transform the nature of the Philippine economy, and that Japanese capital, technical know-how, and managerial supervision could allow the transformation to be carried out relatively painlessly by raising crops such as cotton for which Japan was currently dependent on more remote, perhaps more expensive, and probably less reliable sources. In exchange, Japan was certainly capable of supplying the Philippines with all the manufactured goods then being purchased at high prices from the United States.[27]

In the fall of 1935, word reached the Philippines from Washington that the difficult and delicate textile issue was being handled at the diplomatic level and that the Philippine Legislature, much to its relief, need not take any action. On October 19, 1935, the Department of State announced a "Gentlemen's Agreement" with Japan covering the textile situation in the Philippines. The agreement provided that, in return for no increase in the Philippine tariff on cotton piece-goods, the Japanese would voluntarily limit imports of Japanese cotton piece-goods for two years, beginning August 1, 1935, to 45 million square meters annually.[28] The 45 million figure was a compromise between the 24 million square-meter total of 1933 and the 56 million total of 1934. On the surface the compromise seemed to hold benefits for both parties since (1) the Japanese could now be assured that for the first two years of the Commonwealth transition period, which was to begin November 15, 1935, the Philippine Legislature would not pass any restrictive tariff legislation, and (2) the Americans were now equally assured of retaining a significant share of the Philippine cotton-textile market. In fact, thanks to duty-free protection and consumer preference, over the next two years American cotton piece-goods might be worth twice as much as those from Japan, even if the volume of Japanese goods was greater.

Subsequently, however, confidential data from the office of the United States high commissioner demonstrated that the Japanese exceeded their quota by over 12 percent for the total two-year period of the agreement, and that the excess was principally the result of transshipments, that is, material of Japanese origin not shipped directly from Japan to the Philippines. In addition, a fairly large share of the textile trade had been diverted to rayon, which was not covered by the "Gentlemen's Agreement." Before 1935,

maximum total imports of rayon into the Philippines had
never reached 8 million square meters. In 1935 alone,
however, imported rayon piece-goods totaled 14 million
square meters,[29] while from January to May 1936 the total
reached 13,437,240 square meters.[30] For the full year,
1936, the amount of imported rayon climbed to 25 million
square meters, 97 percent of which was of Japanese
manufacture.[31] Thus, in the view of the United States high
commissioner to the Philippines, the position of American
textile interests had not really improved, and he
recommended a much more rigorous, comprehensive, and
enforceable arrangement with the Japanese.

However, the high commissioner's views were
significantly counteracted by a report prepared by two
economic analysts of the United States Tariff Commission.
The conclusion of this very detailed study, which appeared
in February 1937, was that Japanese trade with the
Philippines was not nearly as great as had been represented
and there was on the part of Americans a "general
misconception" regarding the supposed extent of Japanese
gains in the recent past. The report placed the blame for
this misunderstanding on a customs yardstick which had
valued the yen at fifty cents when, with depreciation, it
had actually fallen to twenty-eight cents. For example, it
was argued, insular imports from Japan in 1933 had been
officially reported at the equivalent of $9.5 million, or
13 percent of total Philippine imports for the year, but
subsequent revaluation of the yen reduced the amount to
$5.68 million, or only 8 percent of total imports.[32]

Actually, according to the views of these Tariff
Commission experts, such Japanese increases as there were
had come about at the expense of other nations. For, while
Japan had displaced the United States as the principal
supplier to the Philippines of cotton textiles, the total
trade volume of both the United States and Japan had risen

while that of all other countries had declined. The net
effect of this report in Washington was to vitiate the
concerns of High Commissioner Paul McNutt and bring about an
extension of the "Gentlemen's Agreement" for an additional
year beyond the two-year period for which it had been
originally negotiated.

In 1938 and 1939 the "Gentlemen's Agreement" was again
extended, each time for one year, and the quota of
45 million square meters of cotton piece-goods from Japan
was retained. The real success of the "Gentlemen's
Agreement," however, could probably not be measured
accurately since Japanese exports were increasingly affected
by the demands on Japanese factories of the war effort in
China and because Chinese shopkeepers in the Philippines had
renewed their resistance to handling Japanese products. For
example, Japan's share of the total Philippine import trade
fell to less than 10 percent in 1938, with the value of
cotton piece-goods only 19 percent of the total imported
into the Philippines, 8 million square meters less than the
limit set by the agreement.[33] Similarly, although in 1938
Japan still supplied the Philippines with 86.2 percent of
its rayon imports, there was a sharp drop toward the end of
the year and during the first three months of 1939, and a
concurrent rise in the sales of American rayon, which by
March 1939 exceeded the combined total of imports from both
Japan and Hong Kong (the point from which transshipments
were often made).[34]

It is important, of course, to understand that at no
time had the textile agreements with the United States in
any way affected the continuing long-range efforts of the
Japanese to bring about closer economic ties with the
Philippines. Trade delegations and parliamentary missions
arrived in the Philippines from Japan with increasing
frequency. Friendly associations between Filipino
businessmen and politicians and their Japanese counterparts

were persistently encouraged. Filipinos were urged to visit Japan and when they did they were given the warmest possible receptions. All of these activities had an impact in the Philippines and there was everywhere an increasing awareness of Japan. Obviously Japan's insightful analysis of the motivations of the American Congress in passing the Tydings-McDuffie Act played a crucial role in its increasing determination to advance economic ties with the Philippines.

That all of these efforts were beginning to have salutary results seemed apparent in statistics released in May 1940. These figures showed that, although exports from Japan to the Philippines had decreased, Japanese imports from the Philippines rose from a figure of 36 million yen in 1938 to 49 million yen in 1939.[35] This drastic revision in the traditional unfavorable balance of trade for the Philippines seemed to some to be proof of the wisdom of those Japanese who had insisted that the Filipinos could find a dependable market for their natural products in Japan.

In reality, however, the war situation had seriously transformed the nature of the market, making it possible for the Philippines to secure some momentary advantages which had not been available before. Japan's domestic needs were greater than ever as she pressed her war machine into high gear and pushed her productivity levels to record highs. Japan's traditional sources of raw materials, such as Malaya and the Netherlands East Indies, were being affected by the participation of the respective mother countries in the European war, and a far greater share of their crop production was being absorbed accordingly. Shipping bottoms and shipping facilities were at a premium. Prices that were traditionally lower in other Southeast Asian countries than in the Philippines began to equalize, and in a war situation, with the need to stockpile, price was no longer a significant consideration. Another factor which contributed

to the increase of Philippine sales to Japan was Japan's
function as an entrepôt for transshipments of raw products
to her Axis partner, Germany, many of whose needs were met
via the Trans-Siberian Railway right up to the German
invasion of Russia. For all of these reasons, products such
as sugar, copra, and coconut oil, which the Philippines had
always wanted to sell to Japan and which the Japanese had
always said they would buy if they could, were at long last
finding their way into the Japanese market.

In December of 1940 the newly appointed Japanese consul
general, Niiro Katsumi, arrived in Manila to take up his
post. Of special significance to Japan's economic interest
in the Philippines, perhaps, was the fact that Niiro
received his appointment directly after having served as
chief of the first section of the Bureau of Commerce in the
Foreign Ministry where he was recognized as an expert on
trade and industry. On his arrival in Manila, Niiro told
the Philippine press while "smiling and back-patting" that
he had only one determination: "to work for the promotion of
cultural, trade and friendly relations between the
Philippines and Japan."[36] This commitment of Niiro was
further evidenced some six months later when he requested
from the Foreign Ministry subsidies of at least ten thousand
yen each for the Japanese Chamber of Commerce of Manila and
for the Committee on Emergency Countermeasures, a body made
up of local Japanese specially organized to combat numerous
anti-Japanese measures which began seriously to affect the
welfare of the Japanese community in the Philippines during
1941. Niiro further urged that in case the ministry should
decide only to provide a subsidy for the Japanese Chamber of
Commerce, the amount should be twenty thousand yen.[37]

As war clouds lowered over the Pacific in 1941,
economic pressures on Japanese-Philippine trade increased
substantially, principally, of course, as a result of
worsening United States-Japanese relations. Export

regulations covering all exports from the Philippines were put into effect May 29, 1941, and an order freezing all Japanese assets there was decreed on July 26, 1941. Yet these new restrictions were only the latest and most severe of a series of ostensible curbs that had been placed on Japanese economic activities in the islands prior to 1941, and none of the previously enacted obstacles had either seriously impeded the growth of Japanese economic interests in the Philippines or had discouraged the Japanese from their long-range economic goals. One is necessarily impressed by the business ingenuity, skill, and perseverance of the Japanese community there. Moreover, of particular significance to the sustained momentum of Japan's economic effort in the Philippines was the success of the traders and merchants on one hand and of the consular staff on the other in working, not only in the closest concert with each other, but in evolving mutually rewarding relationships with their Filipino opposites both in business and government.

Clearly America's permissive colonialism, as it is interpreted by this writer, also facilitated Japan's economic advancement in the prewar Philippines. From the onset of American colonial rule, American domestic economic interests took precedence over the limited American investment in, and trade with, the Philippines. Moreover, the relative weakness of the power of the United States in the Pacific, both economic and military, resulted in a desire to achieve accommodation with Japan whenever possible.[38] In addition, "the reluctant colonial mentor" syndrome, which before and after the Tydings-McDuffie Act burdened the American psyche in general and most American officials in the Philippines specifically, engendered guilt feelings which the Japanese fully recognized and from which they were well prepared to profit.

Notes

1. David R. Sturtevant, *Popular Uprisings in the Philippines: 1840-1940* (Ithaca: Cornell University Press, 1976), 59.

2. K. Watanabe, "History of Japanese Trade in the Philippines," in *The Philippine-Japanese Yearbook and Business Directory* (Manila: M. Farolan, 1938), 1:323.

3. Ibid.

4. *Facts and Figures About Philippine Island Trade with Japan* (Manila: Department of Commerce and Agriculture, 1935).

5. Catherine Porter, *Crisis in the Philippines* (New York: Alfred Knopf, 1942), 84.

6. S. V. Epistola, "The Japanese Adventure in the Philippines," in *Progress* (Manila: Manila Times Publishing, 1960), 104.

7. U.S. National Archives, Bureau of Insular Affairs, Record Group 350, 6144-160A (hereafter cited as BIA, plus file number).

8. Act no. 4003, chap. II, sec. 20.

9. Atherton Report on Wood-Forbes Mission, 15 Nov. 1921, BIA, 22639A-56A.

10. Helmut G. Callis, *Foreign Capital in Southeast Asia* (New York: Institute of Pacific Relations, 1942), 20.

11. These letters are found in the personal papers of Manuel L. Quezon, National Library, Manila, Philippines; microfilm copies of the Quezon Papers are

available in the Michigan Historical Collections, Ann
Arbor.

12. "The extent to which the Philippine economy became
dependent upon free trade with the United States is
suggested by the fact that during the decade ending in
1937 the Islands shipped to the United States between
75 and 87 percent of its total annual exports and
obtained from the United States between 59 and
65 percent of its total annual imports." J[oseph]
Ralston Hayden, *The Philippines: A Study in National
Development* (New York: Macmillan, 1942), 789.

13. BIA, 6144-174B, 7 Nov. 1932.

14. Ibid., 8 Nov. 1932.

15. *Manila Tribune*, 1 Apr. 1933.

16. Ibid., 26 Jan. 1934.

17. Quoted in Maj. William H. Anderson, *The Philippine
Problem* (New York: G. P. Putnam's Sons, 1939), 272.

18. Imports of cotton cloth from the United States declined
from 68 million square meters in 1933 to 43 million
square meters in 1934, while imports from Japan rose
from 24 million square meters in 1933 to 56 million
square meters in 1934 (Ethel B. Dietrich, "Closing
Doors Against Japan," *Far Eastern Survey* 7, no. 16
[10 Aug. 1938]:181-87). For a detailed chronicle of
United States-Philippine economic relations in the
period after the passage of the Tydings-McDuffie Act,
see Sidney Fine, *Frank Murphy: The New Deal Years*
(Chicago: University of Chicago Press, 1979), 132-54.

19. *New York Herald Tribune*, 18 Feb. 1934.

20. *New York Times*, 11 Aug. 1935.

21. Thomas Ireland, *War Clouds in the Skies of the Far East*
(East Rutherford, N.J.: Putnam, 1935), 345.

22. Members of the committee were Democratic Senators Carl
    Hayden of Arizona, William G. McAdoo of California,
    Kenneth McKellar of Tennessee, and Millard Tydings of
    Maryland, and Republican Senator Ernest W. Gibson of
    Vermont. Senators McKellar and Gibson, who had voted
    for the Tydings-McDuffie Act, indicated on their return
    to the United States that they had had a change of
    heart. Said Senator Gibson, who became a vigorous
    retentionist, "Japan is moving in as we are moving out"
    (*New York Times*, 10 May 1935).

23. Grayson Kirk, *Philippine Independence: Motives,
    Problems and Prospects* (New York: Farrar, 1936),
    128-32.

24. Ibid., 133.

25. *New York Times*, 11 Aug. 1935.

26. Despatch no. 1371, 27 June 1935, from United States
    Embassy, Tokyo (BIA, 6144-203B).

27. During the World War II Japanese occupation of the
    Philippines, the Japanese attempted to raise cotton on
    lands that traditionally had been used for the planting
    of sugar, claiming that sugar production had depended
    on an artificially created foreign market.
    Unfortunately, the experiment was a miserable failure
    because of popular indifference on the part of the
    Filipinos, a poor choice of lands on which to cultivate
    cotton, weather obstacles, and the ravages of pests and
    insects.

28. The agreement was retroactive only to August 1935, so
    that the actual total of Japanese cotton-textiles
    imported into the Philippines during 1935 reached an
    all-time high of 72 million square meters (Dietrich,
    "Closing Doors").

29. *Report on Conditions and Affairs in the Philippine
    Islands During the Quarter Ending June 20, 1937*, 61.

30. G. C. Monden, "Is Japan Playing Ball With Us?" *The Commonwealth Fortnightly*, September 1937, 29.

31. *Report on Conditions*, 61.

32. *United States-Philippine Trade With Special Reference to the Independence Act and Other Recent Legislation*, U.S. Tariff Commission, Report no. 118, 2d ser. (Washington, D.C.: Government Printing Office, 1937), 30.

33. F. T. Merrill, "The Outlook for Philippine Independence," *Foreign Policy Reports* 15 (15 Sept. 1939):159-61.

34. *Philippines Herald*, Aug. 1939.

35. Ibid., 15 May 1940.

36. *Philippines Free Press*, 26 Dec. 1940, p. 25.

37. Japan, Ministry of Foreign Affairs, E.2.6.0.1-23, 18 June 1941. Subsidies from the Foreign Office in Tokyo to the Japanese Chamber of Commerce of Manila had begun with one thousand yen for the year 1937.

38. "Quezon and [High Commissioner] Murphy . . . were determined not to provoke Japan. . . . The policy of nonconfrontation that they adopted continued without change until the Japanese attacked the Philippines" (Fine, *Frank Murphy*, 111).

THE PHILIPPINES AS AN EXAMPLE OF THE FORD
MOTOR COMPANY'S MULTINATIONAL STRATEGY

Harold C. Livesay

My purpose in this paper is to discuss the Ford Motor
Company's operations in the Philippines from the perspective
of the company itself. This should not be interpreted as an
advance apology for a defense of the company, for it lies
beyond my competence to decide what policy toward industrial
products--and their manufacture or importation--would best
serve the interests of the Philippine people. Ultimately,
on the resolution of that question hinges the determination
of whether the company's presence contributes to the
country's general welfare.

The Ford case merits consideration because it not only
provides an example of a multinational at work, but also
because it highlights questions that confront any lesser-
developed country like the Philippines, with its
overwhelmingly agricultural economy, feeble industrial
sector, surplus population, and the crippling limitation of
inadequate indigenous supplies of technology, capital, and
managerial skills that effectively preclude the creation of
a viable manufacturing capacity using its own resources
alone. The Philippines and countries like it face these
questions regardless of whether their political system
functions as a corrupt dictatorship, a social democracy, or
as some variation in between. No serious political
economist of whom I am aware, regardless of political
persuasion, suggests that any nation can achieve a decent

standard of living without reliable supplies of some
manufactured goods, obtained at an affordable price. How to
obtain the goods is a dilemma; Ford's operations in
Southeast Asia provide one resolution. I do not suggest
that it is the best, but it provides a real, rather than
theoretical, basis for consideration.

The significance of Ford's Philippine activities goes
far beyond the simple interaction of a big, powerful company
with a small, weak nation, for the company's product, the
motor vehicle, is a hieroglyphic representing a complex web,
any strand of which a competent Filipinist could follow back
to the roots of Philippine history. The decision to rely on
the motor vehicle as a fundamental component of the
country's transportation system, regardless of when taken
and by whom, grew out of and impacted upon imperialism and
independence; law enforcement and guerrilla warfare;
commercial and subsistence agriculture; nationalism,
regionalism, and tribalism; urbanization and rural
depopulation; educational opportunities, goals, and methods;
social stratification and mobility; and economic self-
sufficiency or dependency.

It is this last strand, the impact of the automobile on
the national economic policy relating to both domestic and
foreign trade, that I want to grasp here, for the automobile
inevitably has an elaborate underlying logic of its own that
dictates a confrontation with a series of hard choices, each
with benefits and consequences that ripple through society.
The automobile is not something one can simply have and
enjoy, like a painting, or a brook gurgling through the
backyard; it necessitates an involved infrastructure of
highways on which to run it, gasoline to fuel it, mechanics
and parts to repair it, and docks at which to load and
unload it, each representing capital and skills invariably
in short supply in a society like that of the Philippines.

The decision to introduce the automobile into widespread use (as opposed to keeping it a toy for the rich) presumably resulted from the conclusion that the benefits of a flexible (as compared to rail, the most likely alternative), low-cost (in terms of the original outlay of domestic capital) form of transportation outweighed the costs. The costs, however, invariably prove greater than original estimates and some of them defy easy quantification. Not only does operation of the motor vehicle require the infrastructure discussed above, but it soon becomes, as Americans know better than any, an addiction leading to massive dependency and the need for ever-increasing supplies. The net effect of these inherent traits of the motor vehicle is to force upon countries like the Philippines an apparent choice between tying up scarce domestic capital and skills in automotive and associated industries, or surrendering some measure of sovereignty by buying abroad. In fact, creating a home industry usually involves prohibitive costs, so the choice ultimately boils down to importation on the one hand or inducement of a foreign company to set up assembly or manufacturing plants on the other. Most developing countries strongly prefer the latter, for importation smacks of knuckling under to imperialism and drains scarce foreign exchange. Assembly or manufacturing, especially the latter, may bring investment, employment, and technical training to the home economy.

Persuading foreign companies to assemble is difficult; inducing them to manufacture is more difficult still, because the effective demand of the local market rarely justifies the massive investment necessary for even rudimentary manufacturing facilities for so technically complex a product as the automobile. Indonesia, for all its hundred-million-plus people, offers a less promising arena for investment in automobile manufacturing than Norway, with a population a fortieth as large. As Professor Mira Wilkins has impeccably documented, poorer nations throughout the twentieth century have had to weigh the benefits of barring imports and forcing foreign companies to assemble or manufacture against the risk that foreign suppliers might respond to such legislation by withdrawing altogether, with consequences that can be seen, for example, in contemporary Cuba.[1] A national commitment to the motor vehicle, then, whether resulting from such well-intentioned strategies as facilitating economic growth through improved transportation and communication, or multiplying the country's educational resources, or from more sinister motives such as strengthening the central government's capacity to suppress rebellion, breaking down regionalism, or enforcing cultural homogeneity, has the accompanying effect of decreasing the country's economic self-sufficiency. The choice, then, lies not between independence or dependency, but between types of dependency and their associated costs, among which a purely economic cost may be the least punitive.

In the elaborate *pas de deux* danced by automobile companies and potential host countries, the manufacturers enjoy manifold advantages, superior experience and continuity of governance not least among them. In the small family of producers willing and able to operate in the Philippines, no member has a longer history of successful international operations than the Ford Motor Company. Ford made its first sale outside the United States in 1904. By 1908, a contemporary journal observed, a Ford owner could drive his vehicle around the world and have it serviced every night in a Ford-authorized garage. Ford's overseas operations followed, indeed established, the pattern described by Professor Wilkins, first exporting finished vehicles to foreign dealers, then parts to foreign assembly plants, and, finally, moving gradually to local manufacture of components when required by law and justified by market volume. The Model T, the vehicle that carried the Ford Motor Company from its insignificant beginnings in the Piquette Avenue factory in Detroit in 1903 to a global

empire by the 1920s, proved ideally suited to motoring
conditions in underdeveloped corners of the world and
remained so long after it had become obsolete in the United
States. With its high clearance (invaluable on the deeply
rutted tracks that passed for roads in much of the world),
its planetary transmission that allowed shifting from
forward to reverse without reducing power (ideal for rocking
out of mudholes), its simple design that allowed for easy
assembly and repair (the entire vehicle could be
disassembled to its constituent parts in two or three hours
using only the screwdriver, pliers, and adjustable wrench
that came in the car's tool kit), and its easy
convertibility from passenger to freight vehicle, the "Tin
Lizzie" swiftly became, as Henry Ford anticipated, the first
"worldwide car."

By 1914, the Philippines, too, had become part of
Ford's domain, as imported Model T's met the needs of the
American army of occupation and the American "colony" of ten
to twenty thousand people. In 1928, Ford opened a sales and
service branch in Shanghai to supply China, French
Indochina, and the Philippines. After World War II, the
company opened a small assembly plant in Manila (1946). The
plant was sold in 1949 to Mantrade, a local dealership,
which continued assembling Ford cars until 1967 when the
company reacquired the property. Since 1969, the company
has expanded its capacity, accepting without complaint (as
far as the records reveal) the 1973 law that revoked foreign
ownership of land in the Philippines. The necessity to
build on leasehold rather than freehold land has proven no
deterrent to further investment.

From the outset, Ford's local assembler, acting under
orders from Detroit, purchased as many components as
possible from local suppliers. Given the state of the art
in the Philippine industrial sector, these purchases were of
necessity limited to rudimentary products such as seat

padding and finished wood items; the more sophisticated
elements came from the United States, Canada, Great Britain,
Australia, and New Zealand. Such purchasing policies smack
of economic imperialism, suggesting that the company's
purpose was to restrict local producers to high-bulk, low-
profit items while retaining for itself the exclusive
franchise for expensive components, thus maximizing profit,
perpetuating dependence, and precluding the development of
local competitors. Applied to Henry Ford, however, such an
analysis is facile and mistaken. Ford had, in the
understatement of the *New York Herald-Tribune*, "his share of
odd notions," some of them bizarre and a few, such as his
anti-Semitism, downright vicious. He was, nevertheless, an
extraordinarily sophisticated economist, despite a lack of,
and indeed a contempt for, formal training in the subject.
Long before Keynes, Ford understood the relationship between
factory wages and effective demand. Only he, Billy Durant,
and Ransom E. Olds, among hundreds of fledgling
entrepreneurs, foresaw the automobile as a mass, rather than
a luxury, consumer good, and single-handedly demonstrated
the validity of his perception that the car market had an
explosive elasticity of demand. In foreign trade Ford
remained a dedicated, die-hard free-trader throughout his
life, arguing even before World War I that the United States
"should step forward boldly and lead the world toward freer
trade" because "people cannot keep buying from us unless we
buy from them, and unless international trade can go on, our
business will stagnate here at home."

Ford also thought that policies aimed at keeping
backward nations in a state of dependency were folly at its
most short-sighted. In the 1920s he repeatedly declared,
"We ought to wish for each nation as large a degree of self-
support as possible." Far from keeping "them dependent upon
us for what we manufacture, we should wish them to learn to
manufacture themselves and build up a solidly founded
civilization."[2] By the 1920s, Ford had translated this

philosophy into investment in manufacturing and assembly facilities on six continents. These investments were profit-motivated, to be sure, but reflected a different philosophy and proffered greater local benefits than, for example, the strategy followed by Japanese firms to this day of manufacturing at home to sell abroad.

Henry Ford II, who inherited his grandfather's mantle in 1946, shared many of the elder Ford's views on international business. Believing global industrialization necessary and inevitable, Ford II thought American companies had to involve themselves in the process or face exclusion from world markets. In 1962, speaking of underdeveloped countries, he said, "We must go in with our tools and know-how and help them get the things that they want."[3] Like his grandfather before him, Henry Ford II translated his views into company policy, ordering his subordinates to create plans that would permit the company to continue to operate profitably wherever markets could be found. Different national environments called for different solutions; plans tailored to Europe and Latin America had no relevance for Southeast Asia where in the 1960s the company sought a strategy that would secure two objectives: first, to satisfy the demands of emerging countries that the company manufacture locally despite the fact that no single market outside Australia justified the necessary investment; second, to create a going concern on the periphery of that elusive chimera that had dazzled American businessmen since colonial times, the gigantic Chinese market, there to await the happy day when the gates might swing open and the Great Wall be breached.

On February 2, 1971, Ford's Asia-Pacific staff presented its boss with a scheme designed to achieve these objectives. Known as the "Complementation Plan," it called for the establishment of manufacturing plants in countries throughout the region, each concentrating on one or two components tailored to the existing level of industrial proficiency in each country. Taiwan, for example, would furnish gasoline and diesel engines, while the Philippines would manufacture body panels. At the outset, the region would remain dependent on Ford of Europe for such technically demanding parts as axles and transmissions, but this dependency would decline as the technical capacities of the region rose, an evolution that Ford's presence would aid and encourage. Finished components would be cross-hauled to assembly plants scattered throughout the region, from Bombay to Fiji, a complicated supply process to be sure, but one that Ford had perfected in other areas of the world.[4]

All this involved a projected capital expenditure of $150 million in the region by 1980 (typically an underestimate; the budgeted Philippine share, $11 million, turned out to be $40 million), much of it for new manufacturing and assembly facilities, "necessary if Ford is to participate . . . in these countries where government policy is directed toward increasing self-sufficiency."[5] With this network of facilities the company could bypass the problem of the small "size of individual vehicle industries of these countries [which] imposes substantial cost penalties on local manufacture"[6] because "the current size of the total . . . South East Asian markets provides for a much more economic scale of manufacture."[7] In addition, the company hoped to expand the market significantly by introducing a new, low-cost, utility vehicle, more like its ancestral Model T than any of its current products.[8] Spreading the factories around, moreover, would accommodate "the practicalities of the economic and political environment in the area," which required "that benefits of a major industrial undertaking of this nature be spread equitably amongst the participating countries."[9]

The "Complementation Plan," the Ford staff argued, promised the best of both worlds, "being in line with requirements and capacities of the developing countries and, of equal importance, . . . [offering] the best opportunity of improving our competitive position in the markets of each country."[10] "Most of the Governments of these countries," the report concluded cheerfully, "will . . . happily commit to [such] a general arrangement."[11]

Among the happiest governments to "commit" was that of the Philippines. In 1972, the Philippines named the Ford Motor Company as one of five manufacturers (General Motors, Toyota, Volkswagen, and Chrysler were the others) authorized to participate in the "Progressive Car Manufacturing" program. Possibly some chemistry between the Marcos family and the Fords played a role in the decision, but the suggestion that bribery was the crucial factor beggars all but the most paranoid imaginations. Ford and the Philippines had long experience with one another; Ford already had a considerable investment in its Manila assembly plant and had long held a major share of the Philippine market. The "Complementation Plan" promised to expand investment, employment, and export credits for the Philippine economy. These reasons more than sufficed for both sides.

In the 1970s, Ford steadily expanded its investment in the Philippines, adding to the capacity of its Manila assembly plant, building a parts depot nearby, and carrying out the "Complementation Plan" by building a body-panel stamping plant at Mariveles in the Bataan Export Processing Zone, where production began in 1975. Ford employs two thousand people in the Philippines, all but half a dozen of them Philippine nationals. It has the capacity to assemble twenty thousand vehicles a year, all of them equipped with four-cylinder engines with less than 2,000 cc. displacement. The Mariveles plant can turn out one hundred thousand sets of body stampings per year.

In purely statistical terms, the Philippines has fared better from the bargain than has the company. Fierce Japanese competition has devastated Western manufacturers in Southeast Asian markets less protected than the Philippines, often pushing Ford's regional sales volume below the point where the "Complementation Plan" makes economic sense. Consequently, the Mariveles plant has become a truly global supplier, with some of its products appearing from time to time in vehicles assembled in the United States and Europe.

The impact of Ford's operations on Philippine society is harder to measure. The company has created a large number of jobs, most of them providing (so far) reasonably steady employment at pay scales that are dirt cheap by Western standards, but greatly outstrip the coolie wages paid in textile, electronics, and agricultural industries. Ford trains its employees, though for the majority this means bringing them to a semiskilled level at best, often in operations inapplicable to any other industry. The tedium of automobile assembly or manufacturing work needs no elaboration here, although a walk through a sugar-cane field or a day spent picking pineapples might put such industrial work in a different perspective.

Within the ranks of its employees, however, Ford does train a significant minority in skills valuable both to the worker and to the society at large. Computer programmers, accountants, machine repair personnel, and others can and do market skills learned at Ford elsewhere in the Philippine economy, often going to work for, or setting themselves up as, Ford suppliers, a field that expanded rapidly as Ford production grew and local content rose to over 90 percent by the end of the 1970s.[12] In fact, the company worries a great deal more about retaining its skilled Filipino employees than it does about saving the good jobs for the white folks from abroad. Ford has two strong incentives for eliminating foreign-service personnel from its Philippine

72

operations: first, the tax laws in the United States and
Australia, which, together with the higher salaries
necessary to induce foreign-service personnel to go to the
Philippines and stay there long enough to be effective, make
such people ten times as expensive as local talent;[13]
second, relations with the host government and society.
Around the world, for the simple reason that it finds such a
policy good business, Ford tries to minimize its "American"
character and convince host societies that it is, for all
practical purposes, a local company. Few arguments serve
this end as well as a visible management of local origin.
Consequently in the 1970s Ford reduced the number of non-
Filipino employees in the country from thirty to three.

On the whole, Ford's presence has contributed
significantly to the indigenous skill level, both mechanical
and managerial, of the Philippines. How far and wide these
benefits have diffused in Philippine society is a question
that could also be asked about the benefits of the Ford
payroll. Unfortunately, I cannot answer it in either case.
The export credits generated by Ford's operations could
potentially have great benefit to the country, depending
upon how the government chooses to use them, something
beyond Ford's control. One suspects the Marcos government
has made something less than socially optimal use of them.

Since 1969, Ford's "Complementation Plan" has validated
one of the arguments originally advanced by its proponents.
With its "established network of affiliates," Ford's
planners claimed, the company could "operate as a cohesive
whole," drawing components and supplying vehicles throughout
the region, something that no single country could do
because "the majority of Governments [were] not
administratively sophisticated enough to implement such a
scheme and also because the capacity of the private sector
[was] so limited." Therefore, there was "in fact no body
public or private capable of undertaking the task or co-

ordinating its implementation."[14] By its success in the mid-1970s, Ford presented the Philippines with the possibility of deriving the benefits of a growing industrial sector. Just what these benefits turned out to be and who shared them was a matter determined more by the local government than by the Ford Motor Company.

Unquestionably, the company operates in the Philippines for the selfish reason of making a profit, not only in the Philippines, but throughout the region as well. Without this motivation, there would be no Philippine automobile industry. Whether the country would be better off that way seems arguable, but at least, as far as Ford is concerned, the theoretical proposition may get an empirical test. In the last five or six years, Japanese manufacturers have reduced the company's regional operations to marginal or negative profitability. For Ford, deep in trouble elsewhere in the world, the relatively small markets of Southeast Asia may not justify the investment of enough scarce, expensive capital to retain competitiveness. The company may abandon Southeast Asia entirely, or relinquish it to its Japanese affiliate, Toyo Kogyo.

Ford came to the Philippines originally during the heyday of American imperialism and stayed through the country's emergence as an independent and theoretically democratic state. If it leaves, it will be driven out by "Japan Incorporated," which has succeeded through peaceful means in achieving what military power failed to secure, economic domination of the region. Whatever the pros and cons of Ford's presence, experience elsewhere suggests that Filipinos have fared better at Ford's hands than they will at the hands of the Japanese.

In the long run, however, the question of how much the country benefits from the presence of industrial operations, regardless of ownership, depends upon the Filipinos' ability to govern themselves effectively. Indeed, I would advance

this as general proposition: the behavior and impact of
multinational companies depends upon the abiliy of host
countries' peoples to govern themselves effectively, for
even the most rapacious enterprises can be controlled
through effective exercise of political sovereignty and will
accept such control as long as their operations remain
profitable. On the other hand, firms will not stay if they
cannot make money, regardless of how docile the host
government may be. This, it seems to me, shows both the
dark and bright sides of multinational capitalism: it exists
only to make money, but will settle for that and no more.
Investment rooted in political ideology, however, may
tolerate a lack of profitability, while exacting other, more
expensive forms of tribute.

Notes

1. Mira Wilkins, *American Business Abroad*, 2 vols.
   (Cambridge: Harvard University Press, 1970, 1974).

2. Mira Wilkins and Frank E. Hill, *American Business
   Abroad: Ford on Six Continents* (Detroit: Wayne State
   University Press, 1964), 153.

3. Wilkins and Hill, *American Business Abroad: Ford*, 414.

4. Ford Asia-Pacific and South Africa Group, "1980 Plan:
   Presentation to Mr. Henry Ford II," February 2, 1971.
   Ford Motor Company document supplied to me by Ford
   Asia-Pacific, Melbourne, Australia, hereafter cited as
   "Complementation Plan."

5. "Complementation Plan," 6.

6. Ibid., 7.

7. Ibid., 8.

8. Introduced in 1973, this vehicle, called the "Fiera,"
   proved an instant success. Though little more than a
   motorized tray with wheels and brakes, topped by

interchangeable bodies that provided pickup-truck or van configurations, the Fiera in its early years embodied components shipped to assembly plants from fourteen different countries.

9.   "Complementation Plan," 8.

10.   Ibid., 10.

11.   Ibid., 9.

12.   This figure is not quite as good as it looks, since "local content" is calculated through a complex formula in which export credits count as local content. The actual percentage of Philippine-manufactured components in Philippine-assembled vehicles has, however, risen from about 5 to 50 percent.

13.   Ford's foreign-service personnel belie the "Pukka Sahib" image--not that they don't live well, but the overwhelming majority of them regard assignment to such outposts as the Philippines as a major detour on the career path. Consequently, they shun these assignments whenever they can.

14.   "Complementation Plan," 6.

EXPORT-ORIENTED INDUSTRIALIZATION, THE INTERNATIONAL DIVISION OF LABOR, AND THE RISE OF THE SUBCONTRACT BOURGEOISIE IN THE PHILIPPINES

Robert T. Snow

Recent interest in dependency theory and the political economy of the world system[1] has focused attention on the changing roles which nations play in the global economy, and the consequences of these changes for their domestic class structures. During the past ten years, the role of the Philippines in the world system has shifted considerably due to the rapid growth in manufactured exports. From the beginning of the colonial era to the present day, the Philippines has been integrated into the world market primarily as a source of raw materials for consumption in the West and, more recently, in Japan. Since the late 1960s, government-backed efforts to encourage the manufacture of industrial goods for export have begun to move the Philippines into a new role in the world market.

I am grateful for the critical comments and assistance of a number of readers of an earlier draft, especially Joel Rocamora, Norman Owen, Lim Mah-Hui, Purificacion Quisumbing, Ben Kerkvliet, Bob Stauffer, Scott McNall, Gary Hawes, Dereck Liebenberg, and Peter Smith. Many of these readers continued to disagree with my conclusions, but their comments were invaluable in helping me reach them.

The rapid growth of export-oriented industrialization (EOI), notably in garments and electronics, has begun to transform the Philippines from a seller of primary commodities to a supplier of cheap labor-power on the world market. This transformation has important implications for the external relations of the Philippines with the industrialized nations, notably its former colonial master, the United States, and with other Third World nations seeking to pursue EOI. Internally, it has consequences for the class structure of the Philippines. It fosters a domestic bourgeoisie tied to the world market in new ways, attracts a new type of foreign investor, and creates a new industrial work force dependent upon the export market.

Under the Spanish, American, and Japanese colonial regimes, the economic, political, and social structures of the Philippines were molded in ways which left the country dependent upon powerful outside nations. Since gaining independence from the United States in 1946, the Philippines has continued to be burdened by the fetters of neocolonialism. Both the official statements of the Philippine government and the demands of its critics emphasize the need for the Philippines to be more independent of the two most prominent neocolonial powers, the United States and Japan. Ultimately, the structural changes brought about in the Philippines by the rapid growth of EOI must be seen against this background. This paper shows that EOI has continued the external dependence of the Philippine economy upon the American market. It has also fostered the growth of a new domestic class of Filipino subcontractors whose interests are as closely tied to the United States as were those of the export-crop plantation owners of the past. In short, EOI may have changed the form of the bonds of dependence, but it has not broken them.

While EOI has not made the Philippines less dependent upon the affluent nations, especially the United States, it has introduced a new set of conflicts into Philippine external relations. These conflicts take a number of forms. With the affluent nations, the rapid growth of EOI has brought the Philippine government and Philippine-based export companies into conflict with protectionist groups in the United States and elsewhere. In the past, these groups welcomed the export of Philippine raw materials that were to be turned into manufactured goods in the West and Japan. Tariffs and other trade barriers were low. In the industrialized nations, however, fear of loss of markets, and ultimately loss of jobs, because of inexpensive manufactured exports from the Philippines and other Third World nations has fueled protectionism.

Second, the emergence of the Philippines as an exporter of manufactured goods has brought it into competition with neighboring countries pursuing the same strategy. A number of Asian governments are now trying to outbid each other by offering high incentives and low wages to attract EOI foreign investors. Most recently the Philippines appears to be pitted against Sri Lanka and Indonesia in this arena. Countries are also competing to keep the prices of their goods as low as possible and to receive import quotas from the developed nations that are as large as possible. On this front, the entry of the People's Republic of China into the world export-manufacturing market, especially into the garments market, has caused the Philippines and other Asian nations considerable anxiety due to the cheapness of Chinese labor.

Internally, EOI has several effects on the class and political structure of the Philippines. In terms of the working class, EOI fosters the growth of a new, largely female proletariat. EOI has expanded rapidly in East and Southeast Asia because investors have found this part of the world the most suitable source of cheap labor for types of production which have become too expensive in high-wage

79

countries.[2] The need for a cheap, disciplined, and
productive work force, which initially attracted EOI
investors to the Philippines and other Asian nations,
targets a specific type of worker, namely the young woman.
While precise statistics are difficult to obtain, the
garment and electronics industries combined employed over a
half million women in the Philippines by the late 1970s.[3]
If this estimate is correct, EOI would account for over half
of the women employed in manufacturing in the Philippines.
While this paper will not focus on the importance of this
new female workforce,[4] it should be apparent that the
creation of a new group of this type, often in concentrated
areas around Manila or the export processing zones, has an
impact on the women themselves and on their communities. If
changes in world market demand for EOI products should lead
to large-scale layoffs of these workers, and there is some
evidence that this may already be the case, they could
become a new political variable on the Philippine domestic
scene.

In terms of the industrial elite, EOI promotes a new
role for both Filipino and foreign corporations. The
primary commodities which form the backbone of Philippine
exports have been produced by plantations and mines owned by
Filipino and foreign investors. These groups have used
their influence to attempt to prevent trade barriers in both
the Philippines and in the buyer countries that might
restrict the flow of these commodities. During the 1950s
and 1960s, the Philippine government encouraged import-
substitution industrialization (ISI) to produce goods to
supply the domestic market. Again, both Filipino and
foreign investors, sometimes with ties to primary commodity
producers and sometimes without, established "infant
industries" protected by high tariff walls that severely
limited competition from goods produced outside the country.
The ISI group remains important in the Philippines today,

exerting pressure on the government to continue some degree
of tariff protection for these industries.

EOI, modeled on the apparent successes of Hong Kong,
Taiwan, Korea, and Singapore, has been encouraged by the
Philippine government since the late 1960s. In EOI the
state offers incentives for investment in labor-intensive
industries, employing extremely low-wage semiskilled
workers, whose products have a potential overseas market
because of their relatively low labor cost. The tariff
structure required by both Filipino and foreign EOI
producers is much closer to that of the plantation and mine
owners than to the high protectionist barriers erected for
ISI industrialists. Raw materials (for example, high-
quality textiles for garments or components for electronics)
must be allowed entry into the country with few or no
tariffs, and finished products must face few tariffs upon
leaving the Philippines or entering the buyer country.
These conditions are most easily met by enclaves such as
export processing zones or bonded areas. The Philippine
government has established such sites since 1969. However,
further growth of EOI can be expected to produce increasing
friction between ISI and EOI groups over the issue of tariff
and tax regulations. It should be kept in mind that both
Filipino and foreign corporations have invested in ISI and
EOI. This is not a conflict *between* a national bourgeoisie
and foreign investors.

It is also important to realize that the rise of EOI
can bring foreign corporations into conflict with each
other. The foreign corporations that invest in the
Philippines to produce EOI goods have different interests
from those who came in earlier years to exploit Philippine
raw materials or the domestic market for ISI industrial
goods. EOI producers, requiring, above all, cheap and
productive labor and low tariffs on imports and exports,
have become a new element in Philippine politics. The

81

present Philippine government is particularly anxious to attract additional foreign EOI investment. This fact gives corporations that have already established facilities in the Philippines considerable bargaining power.

While the impact of the rapid growth of EOI is important for the Philippine working class and for foreign investors, in this paper I will focus on the consequences of EOI for what I will term the Filipino "subcontract bourgeoisie." It has frequently been assumed in the literature on EOI that foreign investors, particularly transnational corporations, own the facilities which produce the majority of Third World industrial goods for export. However, recent research indicates that in many parts of the Third World this is not the case. Oxford researcher Angus Hone found that direct foreign investors or multinational firms produced·no more than 10 percent of Asian manufactured exports in the early 1970s. Deepak Nayyar, using somewhat different sources of evidence, puts the figure slightly higher, at 15 percent for Third World countries as a whole. He adds that the percentage of manufactured exports produced in these countries by transnational corporations "has not registered any significant increase since 1966." Both these studies conclude that the great majority of the goods are in fact produced by local firms tied to Western and Japanese companies by one of several sorts of subcontract agreement.[5]

Subcontracting is not a new phenomenon, but it has grown with surprising speed in the past fifteen years.[6] Susumu Watanabe of the International Labour Office provides the most succinct definition of subcontracting:

> A (parent) firm is said to be
> "subcontracting" when it requests another
> independent firm (subcontractor) to
> undertake the whole or part of an order it
> has received instead of doing the work
> itself, while assuming full responsibility

> for the work vis-a-vis the customer.
> Subcontracting differs from the mere
> purchase of ready-made parts and components
> off the shelf in that there is an actual
> contract between the two parties setting out
> the specifications of the order.[7]

Subcontracting is attractive to foreign buyer-corporations
because it eliminates the risks of establishing a direct
subsidiary in a country which, while offering low wages or
other advantages, is unfamiliar or poses high risks. The
threat of nationalization or revolution is minimized for the
foreign corporation, as are the risks of incurring
government and worker wrath in the event that slack demand
or rising wages force layoffs or the closing of a plant. In
short, international subcontracting is the economic
equivalent of the Nixon military doctrine: instead of
risking direct investment for the production of the goods
required, foreign corporations encourage local entrepreneurs
to take the risks, while the foreign buyer-companies
continue to take the majority of the profits.

EOI in the Philippines

> The 'trade' winds which first roiled up in
> Japan--and moved westward to Hong Kong,
> Taiwan, Korea, Singapore--have now touched
> Philippine shores. Considering the export
> record of the past seven years--and the
> track record set by nontraditional exports--
> it may rightly be said that, trade-wise, the
> Philippines is the Asian Country whose time
> has come![8]

Before considering the external and internal impact of
EOI, it is important to understand the speed with which it
has grown. The emphasis on EOI began in the late 1960s when
it became obvious that ISI was stagnating. The growth of

ISI was limited by the small size of the local market for
the relatively expensive types of goods produced, while the
high levels of government protection undercut market
imperatives to operate efficiently. Considerable pressure
from President Marcos and the head of the National Economic
Development Authority, Gerardo Sicat, pushed legislation
encouraging EOI through the Philippine Congress beginning in
1967. To the same end, the Bataan Export Processing Zone
was authorized in 1969.[9] International agencies also
lobbied for EOI in the Philippines. Advice from the United
Nations Industrial Development Office, the United Nations
Development Program, the International Labour Office, and
the World Bank has been consistent in emphasizing the
importance of EOI.[10]

From government statistics, the Philippines has been
quite successful with the EOI strategy to date. As tables 1
and 2 show, by 1977, garments and electronics accounted for
U.S. $374.5 million in export earnings. This represented
12 percent of the value of all Philippine exports ($3,151
million) for that year. In 1978, combined sales of textiles
and garments alone came to $358 million, or almost
60 percent of the sales of the highest single Philippine
export earner, coconut oil ($621 million).[11] Until recently
the policy has been meeting the government's targets for
growth and in some cases exceeding them. From all recent
statements, President Marcos intends to maintain and
increase the Philippine commitment to EOI.[12]

It is important to note, however, that government
export figures may significantly exaggerate the success of
EOI. Most EOI products require a high percentage of
expensive imported materials (for example, electronic
components). If the value of these imported materials was
to be subtracted from government statistics on the export
earnings of EOI products, the picture would be quite
different. Recent information from the Central Bank

TABLE 1

Composition of Philippine Exports
1970, 1974, 1977
(Percentages)

	1970	1974	1977
Traditional exports	89.75	84.70	66.17
Nontraditional exports	9.43	14.87	33.03
(Manufactured)	(8.28)	(12.01)	(22.76)
(Unmanufactured)	(1.15)	(2.86)	(10.27)
Special transactions	0.82	0.43	0.80
TOTAL EXPORTS	100.00	100.00	100.00

Note: "Nontraditional exports" is a term used by the Philippine government to describe export goods other than its traditional raw material and processed exports (especially sugar, coconut products, timber, and minerals).

Source: Sanchez, "Non-traditionals," 170.

indicates that imports of unprocessed and semiprocessed raw materials have increased in recent years and now make up 83 percent of the import payments of the Philippines.[13] The report does not state what percentage of the materials were used in EOI. At a time when the Philippines is suffering from serious balance of payment problems, such reliance upon imported raw materials is a cause for concern.

This caveat aside, the EOI strategy has been seen as a success by the Philippine government and will continue to be an important element in Philippine development plans. All indications are that the continued growth of EOI will have an increasing impact on the role of the Philippines in the world economy, particularly its dependency on its main trading partners, the United States and Japan. Analysis of the changes occurring in this dependency requires an

TABLE 2

Nontraditional Manufactured Products, Ten Lead Exports
1970, 1973, 1977
(FOB Value in U.S. $Million)

		1970	1973	1977	Average Annual Rate of Increase 1970-77
1.	Garments	36.21	57.96	250.24	31.81
2.	Electrical and electronic equipment and components	--	11.32	124.27	∞
3.	Handicrafts	6.52	27.38	75.58	41.91
4.	Chemicals	5.42	10.59	54.58	39.09
5.	Nonmetallic mineral manufactures	3.02	25.16	38.65	43.93
6.	Wood manufactures, excluding plywood, veneer, and lumber	3.95	17.23	35.60	36.90
7.	Food products and beverages	8.25	15.01	30.68	20.64
8.	Machinery and transport equipment	1.06	3.43	27.30	59.06
9.	Cordage, cable, ropes, and twines	1.93	4.55	12.53	30.63
10.	Textile yarn and fabrics	2.81	17.31	12.51	23.78
	SUBTOTAL	69.17	189.94	661.94	38.08
	Others	25.35	36.85	55.04	11.71
	Total Exports of Nontraditional Manufactures	94.52	226.79	716.98	33.57

Source: Sanchez, "Non-traditionals," 173.

examination both of the sources of investment to finance
Philippine EOI and of the markets to which EOI products are
sold.

Investments and EOI

The source of capital to finance EOI is important both
as an indication of the ties between the Philippines and
other nations, and as an indication of changes in the class
structure of the country. Does EOI increase Philippine
dependence on foreign, especially American, investors? Does
it create or weaken a Filipino industrial bourgeoisie?

As mentioned earlier, it has often been assumed that
EOI is a strategy involving heavy reliance on foreign
investors, especially transnational corporations, because of
their control of affluent country markets, their access to
risk capital, and their experience with the requisite
technology. However, as will be shown, domestic
entrepreneurs are a very important factor in Philippine EOI.
Nevertheless, the Philippine government continues to seek
foreign investors for EOI production.

Recent business reports indicate that corporations, at
least those from the United States, are still seeking offshore sites. Rising labor costs in the industrialized
nations, pushed by inflation, continue to pressure firms to
seek Third World production facilities.[14] Offshore
producers of manufactured goods covered by protectionist
quotas in the West and Japan--notably garments, textiles,
and footwear--are being forced to move their overseas
facilities from nations whose quotas have largely been
filled (for example, Korea and Taiwan) to nations with more
open quotas, including the Philippines.[15] Barring serious
changes in the world market or the political stability of
the Philippines, foreign investment in EOI is apt to
continue, although perhaps at a slower rate of growth than
during the boom years just after Martial Law was proclaimed.

Estimates of the importance of foreign investors in
Philippine EOI vary widely. Hone, for example, found that
foreign corporations in the Philippines accounted for just
20 to 25 percent of total manufactured exports in 1971.
More recent government figures place the level higher:
roughly 50 percent of all investment in EOI in 1973 to 1977
came from foreign investors.[16] This estimate is
substantiated by data published by the Board of Investments
(BOI): the BOI statistics for 1971 to 1975 show a steady
rise in the ratio of foreign to domestic investment in firms
approved for special incentives under the Export Incentives
Act (R.A. 6135) of 1970, the principal government attempt to
nurture EOI (see table 3). These statistics indicate that a
large and apparently growing percentage of the investment in
all types of export-oriented production considered together
is foreign investment.

TABLE 3

Proportion of New Foreign Investment
In Export-oriented Industrialization
1971-1975
(Percentage of total equity in firms approved for special
incentives under the Export Incentives
Act [R.A. 6135] of 1970)

Year	Percentage
1971	23.4
1972	24.3
1973	32.6
1974	36.0
1975	49.3
Average	36.8

Source: "Foreign Investments," *Philippine Progress*
          (fourth quarter, 1975):11.

The United States is the largest single foreign investor in the Philippines. At one time, it accounted for 90 percent of all foreign investment in the country, according to *Business Week* estimates. The Philippine government has made considerable effort to diversify the sources of investment to attenuate its dependence upon the United States economy and to some extent has succeeded: "Of the $975 million invested in the country since 1970, 49% has been from U.S. companies, 20% from Japanese, and nearly 10% from Europeans."[17]

Despite a decrease in percentage, it is clear that United States investment in many sectors of the Philippine economy remains high. It is also true that American investment is high in EOI, although precise figures are not available. An examination of the two most important examples of EOI in the Philippines, garments and electronics, provides a partial picture of the investment structure.

While the largest single exporter of garments in the Philippines, Levi Strauss (Phil.), Inc., is an American firm,[18] most garment companies are not U.S.-owned. Statistics from the University of the Philippines Law Center show that just 20.2 percent of all equity in textiles and garments in the "Top 1000" firms is foreign equity.[19] A study by Enrico Paglaban found that "roughly 28 percent of the garment firms are under American control, 23 percent are controlled by other foreigners, and the remainder are Filipino-owned."[20]

Paglaban further notes that American involvement in the sector dates back to the 1930s but became significant only in the 1970s. The influx in the 1970s was pushed by the imposition of quotas in the United States on imports from Japan, Korea, Taiwan, and Hong Kong. The low cost of Philippine labor was also an important incentive. Paglaban found that much of the trade in garments between the United

States and the Philippines is channeled through a consignment or international subcontracting system. Large buyer firms, often American department-store chains such as Sears Roebuck and J.C. Penney, contract with a garment firm in the Philippines to produce items to the buyer's specifications. Recent reports indicate that the Philippine government is encouraging the establishment of "industry villages" or "bonded villages" to permit foreign corporations to bring materials, often cloth for garments, to villages for sewing, processing, or assembly. These villages are to be fenced, duty-free areas specifically designed to sell Philippine labor-power to foreign corporations on a subcontract or consignment basis.[21]

From the trends reported in industry journals and the experience of other Third World nations, it is likely that the percentage of direct foreign investment in the export garment industry in the Philippines will decrease. International subcontracting of various types will expand, encouraging the growth of firms owned and operated by Filipinos.

The dynamics of the electronics industry, unlike those of the garment business, have tended to encourage parent corporations to establish entirely foreign-owned subsidiaries to supply their home-country markets. However, in an increasing number of Asian countries, subcontracting is gaining ground even in electronics.[22] The Philippines has a number of locally owned electronics companies producing for foreign buyer firms.

As of March 1978, the Board of Investments had approved the opening of thirteen foreign-owned electronics companies, of which at least seven were American-owned; however, a total of twenty-three Filipino-owned firms had also been registered.[23] While the report does not give investment statistics for the firms, one can estimate the relative scale of the investment by comparing the estimates given for

"Export Sales at Full Capacity." These figures show that 59 percent of the projected export sales of electronics companies will come from foreign-owned firms, and that 44 percent of electronics export sales will be from American-owned firms alone. If investment is assumed to be roughly proportional to expected export sales, this suggests that the Philippine electronics industry relies heavily on American investment. However, the figures also indicate that Philippine-owned firms account for a healthy 41 percent of electronics export sales.

The importance of Philippine-owned electronics corporations is further demonstrated by export statistics. According to BOI reports, in 1978, 53 percent of Philippine exports of semiconductors, the fastest-growing segment of the local electronics industry, were produced by Filipino companies.[24] This stands in contrast to the experience of many Asian nations during their early years of electronics manufacturing. As with garments, it appears that an increasing amount of the Philippine production for export in electronics is managed on a subcontract or subassembly basis. This trend has parallels in neighboring countries. A recent study of the consumer electronics industry in Asia by Craig Emerson found an increase in subcontracting in countries where the industry had become established (for instance, Korea). As electronics production has developed, countries have acquired greater bargaining power vis-a-vis foreign corporations.[25] In short, evidence from the Philippines and other Asian countries suggests that, despite the high percentage of direct American investment in the Philippine electronics industry at the present time, it may already be close to its peak.

To summarize the argument to this point, it is clear that the expansion of EOI is an important goal of Philippine economic planning and that that goal is, at least to date, being achieved, particularly in garments and electronics.

The role of American investors in these areas is important:
28 percent of garment firms are U.S.-controlled, and, if my
estimate is correct, approximately 45 percent of the
investment in electronics comes from the United States.
However, indications are that Filipino firms producing on a
subcontracting basis in both the garment and electronics
industries are on the increase.

If this trend continues, it will change Philippine
relations with the foreign investors upon whom they have
been dependent. In EOI sectors such as garments and
electronics, where Philippine entrepreneurs find that they
can profitably operate as subcontractors, they will attempt
to persuade the Philippine government to reduce or discard
incentives originally designed to attract direct foreign
investment. Filipino subcontractors will want to control
more of the production themselves. This is already
beginning to occur and has led to tensions between American
and Filipino businesspersons in export and other sectors
because of the government's changes in incentives and
regulations affecting foreigners.[26] In these ways, the new
Filipino EOI-based bourgeoisie may exhibit an independence
usually associated with a national bourgeoisie struggling to
reduce foreign domination of its economy.

Any reductions in incentives or changes in proforeign
regulations, however slight, will displease foreign
investors. However, even if Filipino investors eventually
dominate the ownership of corporations in the export sector,
it is unlikely that this will make them or the economy as a
whole less dependent upon the United States and other
foreign economies. The invisible bonds of subcontract
agreements will replace the more obvious ones of direct
investment. Hone puts the case in rather extreme terms
when, with regard to Asian EOI, he concludes, "The local
capitalists have vanquished the multinational firm, but will
they be able to organize against the U.S. multinational

buyers, the Japanese zaitbatsu houses and the European store groups?"[27]

EOI, Markets, and Trade

Like the shifts in investment patterns, the changes which EOI brings about in the markets and trade of the Philippines affect both the relationship of the country to the world economy and the behavior of the new subcontract bourgeoisie toward the West and Japan. Despite government hopes to the contrary, EOI has deepened Philippine dependence upon its principal market, the United States. While this market dependence continues, the Filipino subcontract bourgeoisie cannot exhibit a truly nationalist, independent stance. It will be a captive class, dependent upon orders from American buyers unless new markets can be found. The diversification of markets for all types of exports has been a key goal of the Philippine government because the current dependence on two markets, the United States and Japan, carries with it the risk of disaster in the event of recession in either of those markets. During the past decade, the dependence of Philippine exports taken as a whole on American markets has been reduced somewhat: for the years 1967-1971, the United States took an annual average of 37.5 percent of Philippine exports; for 1972-1976, that figure fell to 30.2 percent.[28]

The dependence of Philippine EOI goods on the American market, however, is almost twice as great as for Philippine exports as a whole. According to the *Daily News Record* (the primary information source for the apparel industry in the United States), Philippine reliance on the American market is in fact decreasing, but from a position of almost complete dependency: "The share of Philippine apparel exports crossing the Pacific to America dropped to 63 percent in 1977 from almost 80 percent a year or two before and 90 percent before that."[29] *Philippine Development*, the journal of the National Economic and Development Authority, places the level of dependence on the U.S. market somewhat lower:

> The United States still remains the single biggest importer of Philippine garments in spite of the fact that it imposes quotas on all garment items. On the average, it accounted for around 80 percent of the total garments trade in the first half of this decade. In 1975 and 1976 however, this figure declined to 74 and 60 percent respectively, indicating a lessened dependence on a single market and diversification into new, untapped markets. However, exports to the U.S. actually increased by close to 40 percent in 1976. From 1972 to 1976, exports to the United States increased from $32 million to $110 million averaging at [$]48.6 [million] yearly.[30]

Garment exports to the United States are regulated by quota, and the Philippines has usually filled virtually 100 percent of its yearly allocation. The *Daily News Record* pointed out that the 1978 bilateral agreement on garments, which raised the American quota on Philippine garments 30 percent for 1978 but only 3 percent per year for 1979-1982, will mean that the Philippines must either immediately diversify its market for garments from the United States to other nations or face a rapid drop in the expansion of its garment industry, which is currently growing at a rate of 30 percent annually.[31] This means that the dependence on the American garment market is apt to decrease in percentage terms, but not at the initiative of the Philippine government or Filipino garment producers. Even with the tightened quota, the United States will remain the dominant buyer of Philippine garments for the foreseeable future.

In electronics, the market dominance of the United States is again clear. According to Conrado Sanchez, former Governor of the Board of Investments,

> Close to half of all our electronics exports
> go to the United States, 24 percent to
> Western Europe, 8 percent to Japan, and
> another 8 percent to Singapore. . . . In
> 1977 . . . 63 percent of the semiconductors
> made in the Philippines were shipped to the
> United States.[32]

Implications for the EOI Bourgeoisie

While, as mentioned above, the United States takes approximately 30 percent of total Philippine exports, in garments and semiconductors the United States takes double that share. From this it seems reasonable to conclude that, at the upper end of the class spectrum, the rapid growth in EOI in the Philippines is creating a group of industrialists who are *not* dependent on American investment and who are often in fact in competition with American investment, but who *are* heavily dependent on the American market. If members of this EOI bourgeoisie are able to diversify the markets for their products, they may be in a position to benefit from competition between American buyers and those from other countries. This may eventually occur, but there is little to indicate that it will happen soon enough and on a large enough scale to bring a signficant change in this dependent relationship.

For the foreseeable future this new EOI bourgeoisie and the Philippine government which supports it will do everything in their power to pressure the governments of the industrialized nations, especially the United States, to keep their markets open to Philippine EOI goods. In this

effort they will be joined by American and other foreign
investors in the Philippines who are also dependent upon the
export market.[33]   The tensions will be expressed in the form
of Filipino and foreign exporter demands to the affluent-
nation governments rather than friction between these two
groups in the Philippines.

The Subcontract Bourgeoisie

The precise role of the subcontract bourgeoisie in the
shaping of Philippine government policies that affect the
dependence of the Philippines on the United States and other
industrialized nations, especially incentives for foreign
investors, tariff regulations, and tax laws, is in large
part determined by the identity of this group and the power
that it wields within the Philippine political system. Yet,
neither the identity nor the power of the subcontract
bourgeoisie has been studied, and neither can easily be
determined from the available evidence. One can be more
confident in stating who is *not* involved in EOI production.
Reports on the financial dealings of the group of cronies
closest to the Marcos family reveal almost no holdings in
garments or electronics. Instead, investments in banking,
insurance, construction, real estate, hotels, resorts,
agribusiness, and manufacturing for the domestic market
prevail.[34] This is not surprising, given the high rate of
profit to be earned from these sectors, particularly when
the investors have the backing of well-placed persons in the
regime. For the same reason, the risks in such sectors are
relatively low compared with the vagaries of the world
market. Anecdotal information from the Philippines suggests
that subcontracting may be the domain of less politically
and economically influential entrepreneurs, including many
ethnic Chinese, who are willing to accept the risks of
unstable world market-conditions.

While not part of the inner circle close to President
Marcos, these firms are not necessarily small. For example,
a recent article in *Philippine Development* notes, with
respect to garment, textile, and clothing exports, that the
export promotion policies of the government primarily
benefit large corporations:

> One of the major problems of the industry is
> the neglect of the development of small-and-
> medium-scale textile and garment firms. The
> BOI incentives almost always benefit only
> the big firms, which are also the ones that
> easily avail [themselves] of the world
> market quotas.[35]

From the limited information available, Philippine EOI
subcontractors do not appear to be part of the politically
influential circle around President Marcos; however, they
are powerful enough to obtain a portion of the politically
allocated export quotas. Further research is required
before one can come to clear conclusions about the identity
and political importance of the subcontractors.

EOI: Problems for the Future

Most of the discussion above has been based on the
assumption that EOI will continue to flourish in the
Philippines. President Marcos himself has raised the issue
of the continued dependence of the ASEAN nations upon the
West and Japan if the EOI strategy continues to grow in
importance.[36] He stresses the EOI-related problems of
reliance on foreign investors and markets and of growing
inequalities of wealth within the ASEAN nations.

It is, however, quite possible that EOI in the
Philippines will *not* continue to expand, at least during the
coming few years. The world market as a whole and the
Philippines in particular face a difficult period that may
alter the course of EOI and the type of dependence which it

fosters. First, the United States and the world are in a
serious recession. This recession has to cut sharply into
affluent-nation demand for Third World exports.[37] At the
same time, growing unemployment in the industrialized
nations has increased pressures for protectionism to exclude
Third World EOI products. As mentioned above, for some time
this has been the object of Philippine government criticism
of quotas imposed on garments and textiles by the United
States and other affluent nations. The worldwide recession
and growing protectionism have hindered Philippine EOI
efforts.

Another specter closer to home is the possibility that
the Philippines will lose its share of the EOI market to
some of its neighbors. As mentioned earlier, there is
mounting anxiety that other Asian nations, particularly the
People's Republic of China, will be able to undercut
Philippine production costs on the world EOI market. In a
May 1979 article entitled "Peking's Threat," the head of the
Philippine Export Processing Zone Authority stated, "We
anticipate that China will be a major competitor in the
future and they can easily outsell everybody with their
cheap labor."[38] If China, Indonesia, or Sri Lanka proves
more successful than the Philippines in keeping wages low
and productivity high, the Philippines' EOI campaign might
be short-lived.

Finally, even if the Philippine EOI drive can survive
the recession, protectionism, and the threat from neighbors
with cheaper labor, internal political unrest may make the
Philippines a less attractive site for direct foreign
investments and even for subcontract agreements which
require delivery by a specified date. These problems were
brought to the attention of the American business community
in a series of *New York Times* stories during 1979; by
Business Week in an August 1979 article entitled "Problems
in the Philippines Chill an Economic Boom"; and by *Business*

Asia in a September 1979 article entitled "Growing Political Unrest in the Philippines Will Prompt Crackdown."[39] The latter gives the following advice to American corporations operating in the Philippines:

- The immediate threat is criticism of international companies operating in the R.P. from groups in their home countries as Marcos increases repression.

- The medium-range danger is that economic policy shifts aimed at bailing out the martial law regime will run counter to companies' interests.

- The long-range risk is that when Marcos departs, links with the current economic and political elite that have been carefully built may not survive. . . . Should he be forced out, many of the distributors, joint venture partners, and customers connected to Malacanang will become--at best--less effective. They could easily become major liabilities.[40]

Warnings by major business periodicals of the threat of revolution or coup d'etat have a serious adverse effect on a nation's investment climate, and this can only raise doubts in the minds of potential EOI investors or buyer-firms seeking subcontractors. For the first two months of 1979, government sources reported a drop of 36 percent in new American investments compared with the same period one year earlier.[41] More recent information confirms this trend. The decrease in foreign investment made the Philippines, and all the ASEAN governments, more conciliatory towards potential investors.[42]

Other serious problems threatening the government's development strategy include the rapidly increasing cost of imported energy, the already high and still growing $9 billion foreign debt (the debt increased to

U.S. $16 billion by 1982),[43] and the uncertain market for
traditional Philippine commodity exports.[44] As shown above,
Philippine EOI exports grew very rapidly through 1978, but
recent reports indicate that nontraditional exports (largely
made up of EOI manufactures), notably garments, did not do
as well in 1979 as in previous years.[45] At the end of 1979
the Philippine Ministry of Labor reported that 146,000
workers in Metro Manila had been laid off during the first
nine months of the year. The report stated that the garment
and textile industries were the most seriously affected.
Together these two industries accounted for about 80 percent
of the total number of workers dismissed.[46] If this
declining demand for Philippine garments and textiles
continues, large numbers of the women workers who have been
drawn into EOI industries will be forced out. It will also
put pressure on the subcontract bourgeoisie, faced with
fewer buyers on one hand and angry laid-off workers on the
other.

Conclusion

During the 1970s, the role of the Philippines in the
international division of labor changed. The nation began
to evolve from a producer of primary products to a producer
of labor-intensive manufactured goods. EOI grew very
rapidly, particularly in garments and electronics. This
shift in the role of the Philippines in the world market has
certain consequences for Philippine relations with foreign
countries and for the nation's internal class structure.
First, with respect to foreign investment, the Philippines
has always been dominated by American corporations. EOI
does not appear to have significantly altered this: the
United States is still the largest single foreign investor
in both garments and electronics. However, Philippine
corporations operating on a subcontract basis control a
large share of the garment and electronics industries.
While this situation might result from the growing economic

autonomy of Filipino entrepreneurs in EOI, an examination of
foreign trade statistics shows that producers of garments
and electronics for export are even more overwhelmingly
dependent upon the American market than Philippine exports
taken as a whole. Although this dependence appears to be
abating somewhat, at least through the 1970s between two-
thirds and three-quarters of Philippine garments and
electronics exports were still sold to the United States.

This situation has created a Filipino EOI bourgeoisie
which may appear to be nationalistic in terms of resenting
direct foreign investment in the Philippines; however, it
remains dependent upon overseas markets, especially the
American market. This subcontract bourgeoisie may come into
conflict with American and other foreign investors over
Philippine government incentives to attract foreign capital.
Incentives have already been changed, provoking considerable
outcry on the part of foreign corporations that the
government's investment policy is "inconsistent," and that
this constitutes "a major disincentive to potential foreign
investors."[47] There are complaints that the government
keeps changing the "rules of the game."[48] By 1982, economic
pressures had changed this situation in favor of the foreign
investors:

> Representatives of American multinationals
> with substantial investments in the
> Philippines in particular are said to be
> happier in the current business climate--the
> sporadic vested interest campaigns against
> them in the local press which characterised
> previous years have now died down.[49]

Yet, even if this EOI bourgeoisie eventually lobbies
successfully to keep foreign investors out of these sectors,
it is, and will continue for the foreseeable future to be,
directly dependent on the American market. Members of this
class may appear to be nationalists in terms of their

posture towards direct foreign investment, but they will be
compradores with respect to the American market. This
foreign-market dependence increasingly brings them into
conflict with the quotas and rising protectionism of the
industrialized nations.

Finally, the future of Philippine EOI and of the
subcontract bourgeoisie is affected by much broader forces
at work in the world system: recession, protectionism,
Philippine competition with neighboring countries, and the
stability of the Marcos regime itself. There are serious
problems in all these areas. As the risks for direct
foreign investment in the Philippines rise, investors will
rely more and more heavily upon Filipino subcontractors.
This is a direct parallel in the economic sector to the
Nixon doctrine in the military sector: Filipino
entrepreneurs will be put in the position of taking the
risks of investment and the blame for bad conditions for
workers while foreign corporations remain secure, their
hands clean, collecting the lion's share of the profits.

Export-oriented industrialization has altered both the
role that the Philippines plays in the international
division of labor and its internal class structure. It has
changed the form of the dependent relations between the
Philippines and the industrialized nations, especially the
United States, but it has not reduced or broken the bonds of
dependency.

Notes

1. The most widely known theorists in this area are Samir
   Amin, Andre Gunder Frank, and Immanuel Wallerstein,
   although a very large body of literature has grown up
   around them, both agreeing and disagreeing with their
   work. Two of the best critical overviews of the field
   are Gabriel Palma, "Dependency: A Formal Theory of
   Underdevelopment or a Methodology for the Analysis of
   Concrete Situations of Underdevelopment?" *World
   Development* 6, no. 7 (1978): 881-924, which includes a
   thorough bibliography; and Robert Brenner, "The Origins
   of Capitalist Development: A Critique of Neo-Smithian
   Marxism," *New Left Review*, July-August 1977, 25-92.

2. See "Asia's New Bidders for Western Plants," *Business
   Week*, 17 Mar. 1980, 48D-48P.

3. Conrado Sanchez, Jr., "Non-traditionals Spearhead
   Export Growth," *Fookien Times Yearbook* (1978):170-73;
   "Garments: From Rags to Riches," *Philippine
   Development*, 31 July 1978, 18-23.

4. The 1977 *Philippine Statistical Yearbook* (Manila:
   National Economic and Development Authority, 1977), 45,
   states that 772,000 women were employed in
   manufacturing in 1975. For a further discussion of
   export-oriented industrialization and the growth of a
   female labor force, see Myrna Blake, "Asian Women in
   Formal and Non-formal Sectors" (paper prepared for the
   United Nations Asian and Pacific Centre for Women and
   Development, Bangkok, February 1979); Rachael Grossman,
   "Women's Place in the Integrated Circuit," *Southeast*

103

Asia Chronicle, no. 66 (1979):2-17; Linda Lim, "Women and the Redeployment of Industry" (paper prepared for the United Nations Industrial Development Office, Vienna, December 1979); A. Lin Neumann, "Philippine Export Zone: Success at Expense of Women Workers," *Response* (September 1979):12-14; and Robert T. Snow, "Multinational Corporations in Asia: The Labor Intensive Factory," *Bulletin of Concerned Asian Scholars* 11, no. 4 (1979):26-29.

5. Angus Hone, "Multinational Corporations and Multinational Buying Groups: Their Impact on the Growth of Asia's Exports of Manufactures--Myths and Realities," *World Development* 2 (1974):148; Deepak Nayyar, "Transnational Corporations and Manufactured Exports from Poor Countries," *Economic Journal* 88 (March 1978):78. On transnational corporation ownership of production facilities for Third World export goods, see G. K. Heilleiner, "Export Earnings within the Multinational Company Framework," *Far East Trade and Development* (August 1972), and "Manufactured Exports from Less Developed Countries and Multinational Firms," *Economic Journal* 83 (March 1973):21-47.

6. Nayyar, "Transnational Corporations"; Michael Sharpston, "International Subcontracting," *World Development* 4 (1976):333-37.

7. Susumu Watanabe, "International Subcontracting: Employment and Skill Promotion," *International Labor Review* 105, no. 5 (1972):425.

8. Sanchez, "Non-traditionals," 173. At the time Sanchez was governor of the Board of Investments.

9. For further background on the shift to EOI, see Ferdinand Marcos, "Southeast Asia in the Year 2000," *Contemporary Southeast Asia* 1 (May 1979):10-13; Enrico Paglaban, "Philippines: Workers in the Export

Industry," *Pacific Research* 9, nos. 3, 4 (March–June 1978):1-31. Sanchez, "Non-traditionals"; and Robert T. Snow, "Dependent Development and the New Industrial Worker" (Ph.D. diss., Harvard University, 1977).

10. "Free Trade Zones & Industrialization of Asia," *AMPO: Japan-Asia Quarterly Review*, vol. 8, no. 4, and vol. 9, nos. 1, 2 (1977); International Labour Office, *Sharing in Development: A Program of Employment, Equity, and Growth for the Philippines* (Geneva and Manila: International Labour Office, 1974), 109ff.; World Bank, *The Philippines: Priorities and Prospects for Development* (Manila and Washington, D.C.: World Bank, 1976), 23-25; and, of particular significance, Walden Bello, David Kinley, and Elaine Elinson, *Development Debacle: The World Bank in the Philippines* (San Francisco: Institute for Food and Development Policy, 1982).

11. "Patterns and Prospects of Philippine Exports," *Philippine Development*, 15 Apr. 1979, 27.

12. See, for example, "A Discussion with Ferdinand Marcos," *Business Week*, 6 June 1979, 25.

13. "Trade News," *Manila Journal*, 10 Mar. 1980 - 16 Mar. 1980.

14. See, for example, E. T. Smith, "Companies Set Sights on Overseas Sites," *Electronic Business* (May 1979):90-103.

15. *Data Fil*, 1-15 June 1978, 3847.

16. Hone, "Multinational Corporations," 148; Gerardo P. Sicat, "Review of Implement Policies and Programs 1972-1977 and Major Development Thrust in the Next Ten Years," *Fookien Times Yearbook* (1978):156.

17. "Problems in the Philippines Chill an Economic Boom," *Business Week*, 27 Aug. 1979, 51.

18. *Data Fil*, 1-15 May 1978, 3792.

19. *Data Fil*, 1-15 July 1978, 3903.

20. Paglaban, "Philippines: Workers," 6.

21. See "Philippines," *Asia Research Bulletin*, sec. 3
     (February 1980):657-58; and "Bonded Villages," *Ibon--
     Facts and Figures*, 31 Oct. 1979.

22. See Lee Ann Reynis, "The Proliferation of U.S. Firm
     Third World Offshore Sourcing in the Mid-to-late 1960s:
     An Historical and Empirical Study of Factors which
     Occasioned the Location of Production for the
     U.S. Market Abroad" (Ph.D. diss., University of
     Michigan, 1976); and Craig Emerson, "Transnational
     Corporations in the Consumer Electronics Industry of
     Developing ESCAP Countries," *Economic Bulletin for Asia
     and the Pacific* 29, no. 2 (December 1978):50-74.

23. "Electronics Firms Registered Approved by BOI as of
     March, 1979," list obtained from Board of Investments,
     Manila, 1979.

24. Conrado Sanchez, Jr., "Electronics: A Dynamic Export
     Industry in the Philippines" (paper presented at ENEX-
     ASIA meetings, Singapore, 6 November 1978), 6.

25. Emerson, "Transnational Corporations in Consumer
     Electronics," 68.

26. The most celebrated recent cases--involving Avon
     Cosmetics and Continental Can--do not involve the
     export sector but show the tensions between the
     Philippine and foreign business communities. "With the
     government trying harder to attract foreign investment
     to supply jobs, capital inflow, and exports, and to
     reduce protection of industries that have yet to become
     competitive, local companies are likely to be
     vociferous opponents" ("Two Cases Show Problems in

Philippines from Local Opposition," *Business Asia*,
25 May 1979, 164).

27. Hone, "Multinational Corporations," 148.

28. "Patterns and Prospects," *Philippine Development*.

29. "Imports," *Daily News Record*, 9 Oct. 1979, 1.

30. "Garments," *Philippine Development*, 21-22.

31. "Imports," *Daily News Record*.

32. Sanchez, "Electronics," 5.

33. See, for example, "Obstacles to Expanded U.S. Trade and
Investments in Asia-Pacific Region," *AmCham Journal*
(April 1978); and "Pacific Basin Economic Council,
Manila Conference," *AmCham Journal* (July 1978).

34. See "Some are Smarter than Others" (anonymous paper
prepared by "a group of concerned businessmen and
professional managers" in Manila, mimeographed, 1979).

35. "Patterns and Prospects," *Philippine Development*, 23.

36. Marcos, "Southeast Asia."

37. See, for example, Bruce Nussbaum, "Squeezing the
Borrowers," *Far Eastern Economic Review*,
19 Oct. 1979, 73.

38. Adlai J. Amor, "Peking's Threat," *Data Fil*, 16-31 May
1979, 356.

39. "Problems in the Philippines Chill an Economic Boom,"
Business Week, 27 Aug. 1979, 50-54; "Growing Political
Unrest in the Philippines Will Prompt Crackdown,"
Business Asia, 14 Sept. 1979, 289-90.

40. "Growing Political Unrest," *Business Asia*, 289-90.

41. *Data Fil*, 16-31 Mar. 1979, 194.

42. "Southeast Asia: A Siren Song for Foreign Investors,"
Business Week, 28 Feb. 1983, 42.

43. Rodney Tasker, "Support for a Strongman," *Far Eastern Economic Review*, 29 Oct. 1982, 32.

44. Mike Kendall, "Philippines Economy in Trouble," *Honolulu Sunday Advertiser*, 13 Apr. 1980, p. B-3.

45. "Trade News," *Manila Journal*, 10-16 Mar. 1980.

46. "Mass Layoff Hits Metro Manila," *Philippine Times* 9, no. 40 (22 October 1979):1.

47. *Data Fil*, 1-15 Dec. 1978, 4183.

48. *Data Fil*, 16-31 Jan. 1979, 34.

49. Tasker, "Support for a Strongman," B3.

AN ANALYSIS OF REACTIONS OF INVESTORS TO THE
RECENT INVESTMENT CLIMATE IN THE PHILIPPINES

Victor M. Ordoñez

From a number of different perspectives, the present
time is one of crisis for the Philippines and its economy.
Gunnar Myrdal has compared the country to Iran; *Time* has
called it the "Pacific powder keg"; its critics are shouting
louder than before that its doom is imminent.

Indeed, the facts draw very stark lines: the balance-
of-trade deficit estimated for 1979 is $1.6 billion, an all-
time high. The total external debt is likewise at an all-
time high of $8.7 billion, and if the country is to continue
to grow, indeed to survive, considering its import
(especially oil) and industrialization requirements, an
infusion of added investments from the outside is needed.

Interestingly, it is also a period of crisis for the
entire global community. The 1975-1985 decade, though not
as turbulent as the sixties nor as bloody as the war years,
may nevertheless be the most profoundly disturbing decade in
the century. There is simultaneously a mood of
confrontationism and a heightened awareness of greater

This paper was originally presented at a seminar in
November 1979. Although the text has been revised to some
extent, statistical data have not been updated. For sources
of data, see "Bibliographic Note."

interdependency than ever before. Too many hopes, schemes, and formulas of earlier decades have been shattered and there is a creeping weariness and disillusionment as the world watches the energy, population, and equity problems loom larger and larger. Between investing countries and recipient countries there is a growing attitude of mutual distrust--not unfounded in most instances--just when the need for, and mutual opportunity to gain from, investment interdependency is greater than ever.

It is the intention of this paper to look at this mutual distrust on the part of both investors and recipients, to understand its causes (which can often be considered the logical consequence of given economic and policy frameworks), and to help clear the air of the smoke of emotionalism, nationalistic chauvinism, and ideological baggage that so often accompanies discussions of the topic.

The approach attempted is one by a noneconomist addressed to noneconomists, although the matter will require a generous dose of economics and quantitative data. And, because of the rather convoluted title of the paper, it is perhaps best to break it down into the four implied component parts, from the last to the first. Therefore, the first part will deal with the recent climate in the Philippines in general, the second part with the resultant investment climate in particular, the third part with the reactions of foreign investors to this climate, and the fourth part with an analysis of these reactions.

Recent Philippine Climate: An Overview

As with any national economy, that of the Philippines is characterized by bright aspects and dark aspects. I will attempt to lay out both aspects separately and then summarize the Philippine government response to the situation.

On the bright side, the Gross National Product (GNP), while still a modest $24 billion, has grown consistently over the past several years at an annual rate between 5 and 6 percent in real terms, lower than its neighbors in the Association of Southeast Asian Nations (ASEAN), but higher than all other developing nations except Brazil, Tunisia, and Turkey. Per capita income, while also still small, has nevertheless risen from $214 in 1972 to $524 in 1979, more than doubling in that period. The income share of the lower half of the population has improved so that it now earns 29 percent of the total national income compared to 18 percent in 1972.

Prior investments for the future have begun to pay off, so that the funds poured into the Masagana 99 program have made the Philippines a net exporter of rice since 1977 (as late as 1970 the Philippines imported $500 million worth of rice). Infrastructure projects, for which budgets have escalated from $150 million in 1971 to $1.65 billion in 1978, now provide the structures that will be useful in the future.

The Philippine prospects for energy are not as hopeless as they were once thought to be. Present Philippine oil finds are already supplying 15 percent of the requirements of the country, and it is projected that they will supply approximately 50 percent by 1986. In the meantime, alternative forms of energy are rapidly being developed. Hydro and especially geothermal sources of power are expected to provide much of the country's energy in the years to come. Production of alcogas from both sugar and ipil-ipil is being developed. Natural coal is also being mined and abundant reserves are apparently available.

Finally, and still on the bright side, the Philippines has manifested an extraordinary talent for debt management. In 1978 there was in fact a net capital inflow of $66.9 million, and the Philippines has proved its ability

both to seek more loans and to repay its debts. A net
capital outflow was predicted for 1979 due to oil price
increases and other factors that will be discussed below,
but in spite of that the 1979 record shows a 100 percent
increase in public debt repayment and a 65 percent increase
in private debt repayment. The debt-servicing ratio of the
country has remained at least 2 percent below the danger
level of 20 percent set by the World Bank, preserving the
nation's AA credit rating. Prime Minister Cesar Virata has
continued to negotiate extensions of maturities, higher debt
ceilings, additional sources, and better terms from
international financial institutions, indicating high
credibility with lending agencies.

Turning to the dark side, Philippine inflation figures
for November 1979 are running between 20 and 21 percent and
should round out to a figure of about 18 percent inflation
for the year, much higher than the rate of the two preceding
years but lower than the 40 percent inflation figure
registered in 1974. The biggest price increases are in
gasoline, oil, electricity, and water (which will probably
register a 30 percent increase in 1979); services (which
will register about 25 percent); and food, shelter, and
clothing (which will register a 16 or 17 percent increase
over the year). Average wages measured in real terms are
down by about 13 percent since 1972. More importantly, the
rich-poor gap continues to be severe. Even if there has
been some improvement in the income-share picture, the top
5 percent of the population still earns 25 percent of the
national income and controls a whopping 90 percent of total
private assets.

The biggest single factor in inflation, of course, is
the price increase for oil imports. An anticipated
40 percent increase in import bills for 1979 will mean at
least $80 million more than was spent on oil the year
before.

112

As indicated earlier, the trade deficit for 1979 is expected to be $1.6 billion, compared to $1.3 billion in 1978. While oil prices have risen, prices for sugar, copper, and other traditional Philippine exports continue to be depressed. While the export sector recorded a 23 percent growth rate in the first half of 1979, a slackening of Central Bank vigilance has permitted exports to rise by 33 percent.

The total external debt of the country, about half of which is private and half public, is running at approximately $8.7 billion and will be over $9 billion by year end, compared to $8 billion as of last year. This is the equivalent of about one-third of total GNP. About 50 percent of new debts, those recently negotiated for better terms, are used to service older, more expensive debts.

The Philippine government response to this situation was articulated in a speech delivered by President Marcos on September 28, 1979, outlining the major economic policy guidelines of the country for the 1980s. In that particular speech he indicated three cornerstones of this plan for the next decade:

1. An ambitious program for industrializing the country through eleven major projects that will, in effect, require about $6 billion of additional investment.

2. A renewed push for the export orientation of the country, shifting from traditional resource-based export dependence to import-re-export schemes such as those effectively used by the miracle economy countries of Korea, Taiwan, Singapore, and Hong Kong.

3. A program to come as close to self-sufficiency in energy as possible by the end of the 1980s.

In a further elaboration of this program at a meeting with exporters and key officials of the Ministry of Trade, President Marcos explained his industrialization strategy. The country would aim for a further rise in debt ceilings and a further invitation to investors to finance the establishment of major industrialization projects which would, once and for all, liberate the Philippines from its dependence on external markets for both upstream and downstream production. He has opted, in effect, for a direction that would make the Philippine external debt situation worse in order to make it better eventually, rather than to maintain its present difficult state. On the subject of his drive for exports, the president explained that his purpose was, first, to limit the outflow of dollars; second, to optimize production capacity and competitive advantages already existing in the country; and third, to encourage both upstream and downstream integration of present export and trading activities.

The Resultant Investment Climate

In view of the president's drive for industrialization, export, and energy, it is clear that foreign investment will continue to be welcome in the Philippines.

The Marcos administration has traditionally been considered supportive of foreign investment. In fact, his critics have pointed to his desire to protect foreign investment from zealous nationalism and political instability as one of the reasons for which martial law was declared in 1972. In any case, the president did amend the Investment Incentive Act and the Exports Incentives Act in 1973 and 1974 and activated the Export Processing Zone Authority. Included in those amendments are increased incentives for investors and exporters, including tax credits, suspension of capital gains tax, tax holidays, exemptions from export fees and taxes, and so on. The traditional limit on foreign ownership and foreign investment in saturated nonpioneer industries was maintained, but with clear encouragement of stability and incentives for foreign investors in other industries.

As a result, during the period 1972-1974 there was a 350 percent growth in foreign investment compared to a 150 percent growth in domestic investment. By the end of that period, foreign investments rose to 117 percent of domestic investments from an original 60 percent in 1972.

More recently, a drop in dollar reserves within the country became apparent. The target of attracting an additional $500 million annually was not being met. There were a number of reasons for this. First, the outflow of dollars overtook the inflow, largely because of greater import buying and rising inventory levels, in anticipation of price increases due to oil. Second, there was an increase in the rate at which external debts were repaid. Third, a significant amount of local investment capital was leaving the country, purportedly on the grounds of Philippine investment in other countries, although a portion of that must be explained as the salting away of dollars.

Because of this concern for low dollar reserves and because of the announced threefold program of industrialization, export, and energy, the president has explicitly invited and encouraged foreign investment on several occasions. The industrialization program for the decade of the eighties invites investors for eleven major projects: an integrated steel mill, a petrochemical complex, a copper smelter, a phosphatic fertilizer plant, an aluminum smelter, diesel engine manufacture, an integrated pulp and paper industry, an expansion of the cement industry, a rationalization of the coconut industry, the development of nonconventional sources of energy, and fabrication for heavy industry.

The exports thrust received a major boost by the creation in October 1979 of the Bonded Export Manufacturing Warehouse Board, around which the new minister of trade hoped to identify one hundred nontraditional export products, to group manufacturer proponents for each one around a bonded warehouse, and to rationalize their production while simultaneously giving them the duty-free import and tax-free export benefits of a bonded manufacturing warehouse, somewhat analogous to a "mini" export processing zone.

Reactions of Investors

In spite of the open and encouraging investment climate in the Philippines today, there has not been a rapidly increasing foreign investment inflow. Investors take the face value invitations and incentives with a grain of salt and are concerned about past experiences with changing contracts on the one hand and future prospects for long-term stability and ease of implementation on the other.

Foreign firms, though cautious, are still interested, however, and continue to invest while a more subtle love-hate relationship develops between them and the host country.

In 1976, a group of major American, Japanese, and Australian investors in the ASEAN region convened in Manila to discuss a positive strategy for foreign investment under the auspices of The Pacific Forum. In the course of their discussion, their concerns relative to overseas investments emerged. The predominant fear was that of a depreciating or floating contract, according to which the host countries could, by national legislation or executive decree, unilaterally change the terms of agreement "on the grounds of the national self-interest." Of course, when this occurs it becomes a matter of judgment as to whether the original contracts were inherently unjust or whether nationalism was used as an excuse to cover other motives.

Second, investors spoke repeatedly of the "national treatment" provision recommended by the Organization for Economic Cooperation and Development (OECD), according to which foreign investors may avail themselves of the same business privileges as nationals, similar to the status of the Americans in the Philippines prior to the expiration of the Laurel-Langley Treaty in 1974. Investors had difficulty with limits on local borrowings, predetermined debt-to-equity ratios, and a restriction on the limits of their growth.

Third, the investors talked at length about the fairness of the expectation of greater profits where greater risks prevail. The latter included market risks, as in the case of small countries; financial risks, as in the case of inflation, national monetary supply policy, and oil; or political risks, as in the case of nationalization, repatriation, or an overthrow of the regime.

Looking beyond the articulated concerns of the investors, there are a number of deterrents to foreign investment that are rooted, not in the Philippines, but in the home countries of the investors themselves. For example, Korea and neighboring investing countries actively seek investment and trade in the Philippines to take advantage of competitive labor costs, underutilized Philippine export quotas to developed countries, and its aggressive export-growth infrastructure. By contrast, the United States does not have a trade surplus, is not as geographically close to the Philippines, and does not enjoy as high an economic growth rate.

In fact, the United States, which is the major foreign investor in the Philippines, is currently experiencing its own economic crisis. Inflation has made the domestic market more attractive than before and the United States trade deficit calls for curtailment of investments and trade. Moreover, recent government scrutiny of the ethics of multinational corporations abroad and pressure exerted by American labor against its displacement by the developing countries' "sweat-shop" production of goods have played a role in reducing foreign investment. Finally, the energy squeeze in the United States has prompted investors to gird up and retrench domestically rather than expand abroad.

A final comment on the hesitancy of foreign investors in spite of an apparently encouraging investment climate might be made here. The postwar expansionist economy of the United States, which was simultaneously rebuilding Europe and Japan, permitted a foreign-investment orientation to thrive. Since Europe and Japan have not only been rebuilt but have emerged as active competitors, and since the mark and the yen have recently fared better than the dollar, this expansionist attitude no longer exists. On technical and production levels, the rapid development of entirely new industries such as the transportation, communications, and, more recently, electronics industries seems to be a phenomenon of the fifties and sixties that is not repeating itself on the same scale in the seventies and eighties. Third, the American government's policy of deficit spending to generate full employment and provide welfare has resulted in a higher tax structure (promoting its own inflation), an environment which makes foreign investment less inviting.

Analysis of These Reactions

A basic premise of the analysis below must be made explicit at this point. A decision to accept the reality of interdependence must be made. In the years to come the Philippines will be more and more interdependent with other nations from the points of view of finance, energy, and trade. The alternative of absolute sequestration is highly unlikely in view of the present power structure, highly difficult to achieve, and highly undesirable in the eyes of most. China, which best exemplified the sequestration alternative, has now itself articulated a desire for foreign investment. In Burma, another obvious example of sequestration, there is little that can be found to commend the policy.

It follows, then, that foreign investment, together with other forms of foreign capital asset inflow (such as loans, export income, aid, and nonmerchandise trade) will be necessary to support Philippine capital-growth requirements in the future. This investment should be encouraged to grow, but should be accepted *only* in a manner in which the Philippine interests are protected. It is hoped that the many lessons contained in past patterns of foreign investment will be heeded and used to guide policymakers to formulate investment frameworks both satisfactory to investors and protective of the country's interests.

It will in fact be the thesis of this analysis to show that the apparently erratic foreign investment policy of the Philippines has not been the result of whim, but has been to some extent dictated as a logical response to the stages of its economic growth, even though this response often has been delayed by the time lag of polity and the perceptions of policymakers. Therefore, expanding on the framework articulated by Roxas for investment patterns,[1] this analysis will proceed by (1) describing particular socioeconomic stages, (2) looking at the activity of investors and traders in each stage, (3) examining the Philippine government reaction to that investor activity, and (4) looking at the new *modus vivendi* for the investor subsequent to that new investment climate, setting the next socioeconomic stage.

First Stage

This stage dates back to the introduction of foreign goods for trade, which resulted in the polarization of traditional society into the subsistence-level rural class outside the cash economy on the one hand, and the moneyed class with access to external goods through a cash economy on the other. From this second group evolved the investment enclaves of the country. These enclaves, best typified by plantations and mining towns (and in a larger sense by Manila itself), were self-contained systems with political, economic, and social dynamics quite different from those of the countryside around them and in many ways more closely related to and dependent upon the community of the external investor than upon their rural neighbors.

A significant figure in this economic stage was the comprador, usually Chinese, who served as the effective middleman between the large traders from the Asian continent (later from the West) and the Filipino enclave buyers. Slowly the Chinese comprador established a firm hold on the rice and coconut distribution channels in the Philippines in the same way that he controlled tin in Malaysia and rice in Thailand. These same channels were soon used the other way, to supply consumer goods, and before too long even the retail trade was Chinese.

Investment and trading activity took the form of large-scale Philippine importation of necessary food and textiles from outside and exportation of Philippine raw materials for processing. Preferential trade arrangements with the United States in the early part of this century permitted American investors to enjoy prime access to Philippine profit opportunities. In fact, this was so profitable that American domestic producers of beet sugar, vegetable oil, and other commodities eventually lobbied in the United States Congress to grant the colony early independence and install tariff barriers which would make imports from the Philippines less attractive. The Tydings-McDuffie Act of 1934 resulted from this lobbying.

The Philippine government reaction to the growing stranglehold of Chinese compradors and United States investors was an attempt to transfer as much ownership as possible into Filipino hands. Retail trade was nationalized and Filipino ownership prescribed. Compromises were made, however, in industries and activities that required either a foreign market or a foreign provider of a specific technology. For a good number of industries, the 40:60 ratio of foreign to Filipino ownership was introduced.

Even after the Philippines was "granted" independence in 1946, foreign investors and their Filipino counterparts continued to enjoy preferential trade arrangements guaranteed by the Bell Trade Act and the Laurel-Langley Agreement. The period after independence saw the emergence of a "Filipino First" policy, originally enunciated by President Garcia in 1949, involving the nationalization of retail trade and encouragement of Philippines-United States joint ventures, generating a new breed of Filipino entrepreneurs and investment partners while continuing to provide American investors with plenty of opportunity for participation in Philippine growth. This led to the second stage.

Second Stage

In the period immediately following independence, the enclaves and metropolitan centers in the Philippines continued to develop with no significant impact on the noncash, rural sector, which supported itself by expanding the frontiers of its arable land. American and joint-venture investments flourished, and food, textiles, and mass commodities continued to be imported from the United States at preferential rates, with the aid of the dollar inflow from war-damage payments. In 1949, 60 percent of all imports were basic mass-market items from the United States.

American investments and trade continued to grow and traditional exports increased as well.

As war-damage dollars began to dry up, however, government reaction to these investment and trading patterns resulted in a policy of protectionism and import control. Officials soon realized that mere transfer of ownership was not enough, since the power of the enclaves lay not so much in their ownership, but in the way they affected the total economy. Import controls were imposed, with average import taxes rising from 23 percent in 1949 to 36 percent in 1957. The import-control objective was threefold: to keep needed dollar reserves in the country, to protect new local industries, and to develop import-substitution manufacture.

In response to this new climate and the resulting government policies, the manufacturing sector developed very rapidly; in 1950, $23 million were invested in the manufacturing sector, but by 1963 this figure had more than quadrupled, to $110 million. An example of this was the development of the local textile industry, which had produced less than one-sixth of the volume of imported textiles in 1949, but expanded until it was producing four times the imported-textile volume by 1967. Generally, however, manufacturing took the form of value-added assembly of imported components, rather than integrated manufacture. By and large, the greatest beneficiaries of the manufacturing and import-substitution boom continued to be American investors and their Philippine and Chinese counterparts who enjoyed preferential treatment according to the Laurel-Langley Act and who encouraged licensing, patent protection, royalties, and repatriation of dividends.

Third Stage

By the beginning of the 1970s, the level of American investment activity in the Philippines had exceeded the $1 billion mark. Amid cries of nationalism and a threat to

the stability of the present administration, President
Marcos declared martial law in 1972, creating a new
atmosphere of stability for investment activity. Investors
were assured of continuity in their activities, and trade
agreements with Communist, Socialist, and Third World blocs
were initiated to diversify trade markets in view of the
imminent expiration of the Laurel-Langley Agreement.

In the rural sector, which by then had run out of the
frontier lands needed to sustain its traditional life-style
and burgeoning population, the demands of growth had to be
met by more intensive and efficient agriculture rather than
by geographical expansion; fortunately, the rice
technologies generated at this time proved equal to the
task.

Investor activity during the decade of the seventies
was characterized by greater dependence on foreign markets.
Local manufacturing expanded to the point where, instead of
the 60 percent figure of 1949, only 6 percent of imports
were finished mass-market items. Total import figures,
however, continued to rise as demand for energy, machinery,
and industrialization requirements (and luxury goods for the
enclave elite) rose dramatically. The result was a
continuous widening of the trade deficit, so that between
1970 and 1975 a $1.3 billion deficit accumulated.

In the meantime, investors began to realize that pure
import substitution imposed severe limits on growth since
the urban and enclave markets in the Philippines were small
and the rural sector was just beginning to become a consumer
market. As a result, this investment and trade climate
slowly gave rise to a shift from import substitution to
"export substitution," in which manufacture was geared for
export rather than domestic markets. The export of raw
materials was augmented or supplanted by export of
semiprocessed goods (made from the same raw materials) or
new manufactured items, a trade which grew at rates that

overtook the levels of traditional exports. The garment and electronics industries, for example, consistently registered growth rates well over 40 percent during the 1970s.

The supportive government response to this picture is best summarized in the threefold program of President Marcos already described, that is, the promotion of non-resource-based exports by various incentives and by such schemes as export processing zones and bonded manufacturing warehouses; the ambitious drive for industrialization to provide backward and forward integration of manufactures by inviting more foreign investment and higher debt ceilings; and the search for local and alternative sources of energy to reduce the high cost of Philippine dependence on imported oil.

It may still be too early to evaluate reactions to this government policy on investments. The export orientation has recently induced Maidenform, Timex, Texas Instruments, and other labor-intensive companies to establish production facilities in the Philippines. It is the feeling of several economists that export growth in the Philippines is at a take-off stage similar to that experienced by the "miracle growth" countries a decade ago. The demand for bigger markets has generated keen interest on the part of investors who now view the ASEAN nations as an integrated market community rather than five individual country markets. It is difficult to evaluate the so-called spillover effects of export substitution on the total economy; the only evidence of spillover to date is increasing luxury consumption by the elite directly involved with the export enclave and further importation of equipment and machinery for more sophisticated export production capacity. In spite of the lapse of the Laurel-Langley Agreement, contracts drawn up before that time continued to benefit American investors, with the result that, between 1972 and 1975, $400 million more were repatriated. Through the 1970s, for every dollar invested in the Philippines an average profit of $3.80 was

registered, of which about $2.00 were repatriated to the
United States.

Fourth Stage

It would seem that reaction of investors and Philippine
society at large to the recent investment climate will
eventually give shape to a fourth stage of economic
development. President Marcos has made a bold decision to
industrialize heavily, and assuming that the Philippines, in
spite of greater financial risk and exposure, will survive
the severe inflation and recession that face the globe in
the early 1980s, the country should eventually be equipped
with the forward (pulp and paper, copper smelting, oil
refining) and backward (steel, oil, chemical) integration
needed by a healthy and more self-reliant economy. A
diversified trade and investment base will serve as a better
hedge against individual fluctuations in a world of
increasing interdependence but greater bilateral risks.

Most significantly, the polarization between the rural
sector and the enclave sector will have to be resolved
before it reaches crisis proportions. Having reached the
limits of the arable frontiers and having arrived at the
higher productivity achieved by irrigation and improved
technology, the rural sector must now actively integrate
into the trade and investment pattern of the commercial
enclave. Trade and investment patterns that have drawn
resources away from the countryside and into the
metropolitan enclaves must give way to more creative
alternative paradigms for enterprise and capital formation.[2]

More creative patterns of investment activity in this
fourth stage should then emerge, with a much stronger focus
on the rural countryside than ever before. Investors must
develop a greater sensitivity to national aspirations so
that goal congruence can be approximated between these
aspirations and their own investment requirements. As

domestic investors increase their capabilities, foreign investors will no longer be required in areas where they have traditionally operated. Foreign investment will be needed only in the much larger or more complex arenas which, paradoxically, may be the very ones that the national polity will want to continue to own. Foreign investors will begin to view the 250 million people in the ASEAN nations as a market, not just a cheap labor pool for "sweat-shops" supplying the demands of Western consumers.

Ideally, government response to this activity will take the shape of refining incentive schemes to provide satisfactory terms for foreign investors in the few areas in which they will still be needed. Hopefully, the government response will provide a climate of stability and trustworthiness within which foreign investors can be assured that initial commitments will remain valid over agreed-upon durations. Out of this new policy climate should emerge new, jointly forged formulas for the involvement of foreign investment capital. Of course, if the government response proves dysfunctional, the resulting disillusionment of foreign investors will lead to withdrawals and recriminations. These will in turn lead to severe economic dislocations, and--in cases such as the Philippines where involvement is extensive--to outright chaos.

The continued success of foreign investment in the future will depend essentially upon the evolution of new formulas for cooperation. Because outright ownership of major enterprises may not be feasible in the future, foreign investors should look to other formulas for adequate control of their investments, such as those now being tested in China. For example, investors could be given control, plus a percentage of output in kind, rather than ownership; they could retain control of the company and the use of capital equipment; or they could enter into a straight contract with

the host country and receive their returns in the form of
contract fees rather than dividends. New formulas must also
be hammered out in response to the gradually emerging ASEAN
reality, so that ASEAN, rather than national, perspectives
slowly come to the fore; for example, inter-ASEAN investment
may eventually take precedence over Western investment.
Finally, new formulas must be found for the direct
participation of private enterprise and foreign investment
in the task of integrating the enclave and rural sectors, so
that benefits of investment growth do not remain bound in
enclaves but genuinely flow to the countryside.

Conclusion

Only by developing a more enlightened mutual
understanding between foreign investors and their host
country can a new formula for mutually satisfactory
interaction be arrived at in the difficult future. Sincere
efforts at redirection are required of both parties.

On the part of the host country (the Philippines), a
growing consensus on the importance, limitations, and role
of foreign investment must be achieved. The areas,
priorities, and conditions shaping the participation of
foreign investments must manifest itself, not only in
intention and presidential statements, but also at the
operating level of implementing and regulatory agencies.
The host country must also develop a reputation for ethical
and reliable negotiations and agreements in which the
sanctity of the contract, once determined to be just, is
kept inviolate.

On the part of the foreign investor, a greater
sensitivity to national needs must be manifested and a
genuine attempt made to achieve congruence of goals between
corporate stockholders and national development planners in
the host country. The notorious exploitative terms
traditionally foisted upon hosts in the form of dubious

contracts and agreements must become a thing of the past. Previous contract terms can then be understood in the context of a changing environment. New formulas for investment, in terms both satisfactory to investors and equitable to hosts, must constantly be sought.

When both parties come to share a working analysis of old investment patterns and recognize the need for new investment patterns in the future, the apparently impossible task of growth (not just survival) in the turbulent eighties may be achieved after all.

Notes

1. Sixto Roxas, "The Economic and Investment Future of the
    ASEAN Region," in *ASEAN (Association of Southeast Asian
    Nations) and a Positive Strategy for Foreign
    Investment: Report and Papers of a Private Conference
    Organized by the Pacific Forum*, ed. Lloyd R. Vasey,
    Case Studies in Public Policy Implementation and
    Project Management, no. 6 (Honolulu: Pacific Forum,
    1978), 51-70.

2. Experiments testing such creative paradigms have
    already begun. One such experiment is the Bancom
    Institute of Development Technology, a nonprofit
    subsidiary of a group of financial companies
    established to explore human settlements management as
    a private-enterprise activity. Its first major field
    site was Licab, a remote municipality of fourteen
    thousand in Nueva Ecija. There it strove to arrive at
    new formulas for external intervention in bringing a
    community to significant growth targets by combining
    the efficiency of private business with the social
    objectives of improving the quality of life and linking
    the isolated community to the national mainstream.
    Around a theme of profit-for-progress, outside
    expertise was employed to help the community as a whole
    work toward its own prosperity. For details, see
    Victor M. Ordoñez, *Bancom Institute of Development
    Technology* (Honolulu: East-West Center, East-West
    Technology and Development Institute, 1978).

Bibliographic Note

Most of the information in this paper derives from
governmental sources within the Republic of the Philippines,
including the Ministry of Trade (*Statistical Bulletin* of the
Bureau of Foreign Trade), the Central Bank (Census
Statistical Office and National Economic Development
Authority), and President Marcos himself (address before the
University of the Philippines Law Alumni Association,
Manila, 28 September 1979). See also:

Paglaban, Enrico. "Philippines: Workers in the Export
        Industry." *Pacific Research* 9, nos. 3, 4 (March-June
        1978):1-31.

"Philippines: Troubles Closing In." *Far Eastern Economic
        Review*, 29 June 1979.

"The Philippines." *Business Week*, 16 June 1980 (special
        advertising section).

Ordoñez, Victor M. *Bancom Institute of Development
        Technology*. Case Studies in Public Policy
        Implementation and Project Management, no. 6.
        Honolulu: East-West Center, East-West Technology and
        Development Institute, 1978.

Roxas, Sixto. "The Economic and Investment Future of the
        ASEAN Region." In *ASEAN (Association of Southeast
        Asian Nations) and a Positive Strategy for Foreign
        Investment: Report and Papers of a Private Conference
        Organized by the Pacific Forum*, edited by
        Lloyd R. Vasey, 51-70. Honolulu: Pacific Forum, 1978.

Stauffer, Robert. "The Political Economy of a Coup:
        Transnational Linkages and Philippine Political
        Response." *Journal of Peace Research* 11
        (1974):161-77.

TAMING THE AMERICAN MULTINATIONALS

Frank H. Golay

When civil government under the Philippine Commission
replaced the Military Government in 1901, the economy of
America's new colony was prostrate after five years of
rebellion against Spain and war against the United States.
Challenged to get the moribund economy moving, the
commission proposed that economic development be sustained
by the migration of American capital and enterprise to the
Philippines. To induce this migration, the commission urged
Congress to provide liberal access by investors to
Philippine public lands, minerals, and forest resources; to
empower the insular government to extend favorable terms in
chartering corporations and granting franchises to investors
proposing to build railroads, electric utilities, and
communications systems; to authorize the sale of bonds in
the United States to provide funds needed to erect an
appropriate infrastructure of roads, portworks, and other
"public improvements" supporting economic development; to
extend the American national banking system to the colony to
provide an expanding supply of credit to insular
enterprises; and to grant the colony a substantial,
nonreciprocal, tariff preference to ensure a lucrative and
expanding market for insular exports.[1]

The three years beginning with the bitter fight in
early 1899 over ratification of the Treaty of Paris, ceding
Spain's sovereignty over the Philippine Islands to the
United States, witnessed a prolonged struggle in Congress

131

over colonial policy. This encounter between
"retentionists," Republicans for the most part, and
"antiretentionists," predominantly Democrats, saw the former
turn back efforts of the latter to establish an American
commitment to free the Philippines. The confrontation
culminated in passage of the Organic Act of 1902, in which
the antiretentionists were able to establish restrictions
which drastically limited the migration of American capital
and enterprise to the colony.[2]

Ownership of land by corporations was limited to 1,024
hectares (2,500 acres), an area too small to support
extensive development of efficient plantation agriculture.
Moreover, any corporation or member of a corporation engaged
in agriculture was prohibited from participating in any
other corporation engaged in agriculture. Mining claims
were severely limited in surface area, underground rights
were restricted to the space defined by vertical planes
through the surface boundaries, and both individuals and
corporations were limited to a single claim on a mineral
lode or vein. The stringency of constraints in the Organic
Act on access to insular mineral resources was confirmed at
the end of the vigorous mining boom of the 1930s when it was
discovered that all major mines in the islands were working
claims established prior to enactment of the law.[3]
Development of forestry industries was tightly controlled by
term leases and stringent limits on the rate of cutting. As
a result, exploitation of forestry resources at the end of
the American period was limited and was dominated by small-
scale mills supplying local needs.

Congress authorized the sale of $5 million of insular
government bonds in the United States to finance "public
improvements" and for a decade and a half turned a deaf ear
to requests from the Philippine Commission that the limit to
such borrowings be increased. As a result, the principal
part of social overhead investment in the colony prior to

the inauguration of the autonomous Commonwealth in 1935 was
financed out of current revenues of the insular government.
Congressional concern to prevent exploitation by American
capital and enterprise was reflected in strictures imposed
on the insular government in granting franchises for
railroad construction and the operation of electric power
and other utilities. Awareness of this concern was also
reflected in the corporation law enacted by the commission,
which reserved ample regulatory powers to the insular
government. Congress ignored the banking recommendation in
the commission's development "package" and American
commercial banks played a minor role in the island economy
over the period of American rule.

Although Congress proved hostile to a development
strategy based on the migration of American capital and
entrepreneurship to the Philippines, it was willing to
establish preferential access to the American market for
exports from the colony. Initially, the preference was set
at 25 percent of United States duties and was nonreciprocal.
Mutual free trade between the Philippines and the United
States commenced with enactment of the Payne-Aldrich tariff
in 1909, and this policy remained the core of colonial
development strategy for the duration of the American
period.[4]

Congress was willing--antiretentionists and
retentionists alike--to establish mutual free trade because
internal free trade was embedded in the American
Constitution, and the Philippine Islands were territory of
the United States. On the other hand, antirententionists
vigorously opposed the establishment of powerful incentives
to induce the migration of American capital and enterprise
because they feared that an economic interest would
materialize capable of frustrating the independence they
intended to bestow on the Filipinos.

I

Under mutual free trade American investment and
enterprise in the colony expanded slowly and economic
development proceeded at a modest rate. Mutual trade grew
rapidly, however, until virtually two-thirds of the colony's
imports were supplied by the United States, and this country
provided a market for more than four-fifths of Philippine
exports as the end of American rule approached in the
1930s.[5]

Political pressures to free the Philippines accumulated
rapidly during the 1920s as the hard core of
antiretentionist strength was augmented by American
agricultural interests alarmed by the competition of rapidly
expanding imports of insular sugar and coconut products.
Similarly, organized labor was vocal in urging Congress to
halt Filipino emigration to the United States and was
willing to free the colony if this step was necessary to
achieve that goal.

As support for independence surged in the United
States, economists of the executive branch began assembling
economic data on the island economy which would be needed as
Congress drafted independence legislation providing for
economic as well as political disengagement. It is not
surprising that this effort was concerned with the role of
American capital in the development of the colony as
American rule drew to a close. Initial studies of American
investment in the late 1920s and during the 1930s resulted
in estimates that total United States direct investment
increased from $122 million at the end of the 1920s to
$136 million in the mid-1930s and jumped to $175 million by
the end of the decade (see table 1).

Over the brief period analyzed, American direct
investment in export production and processing increased
from 37 percent to 60 percent of total American direct
investment. Much of the rapid expansion of investment in

134

TABLE 1

United States Direct Investment in the Philippines
in Late 1920s and 1930s
(U.S. $million)

Sector		Late 1920s	Mid-1930s	Late 1930s
Manufacturing		44.9	45.4	55.5
Export processing				
industries	36.2	36.9	47.5	
General manufacturing	8.7	8.5	8.0	
Commerce		38.4	18.0	18.0 [d]
Utilities[a]		28.0	37.9 [c]	37.9 [d]
Mining		nrs	7.4 [c]	37.1 [e]
Agricultural and other				
real estate		7.4	19.7	19.3
Miscellaneous		3.3	7.4	4.9
Total		122.0	135.8	172.7
Export sector[b]		43.6	64.0	103.9
Other sectors		78.4	71.8	68.8

Sources: Late 1920s: U.S. Tariff Commission, *U.S.-*
Philippines Trade Relations, Report no. 18, 2d
ser., 62 (estimates of C. C. Howard, U.S. Trade
Commissioner, dated March 9, 1930).

Mid-1930s: U.S. Tariff Commission, *United*
States-Philippine Trade, Report no. 118, 2d
ser., 191 (estimates of J. Bartlett Richards,
U.S. Trade Commissioner, dated June 30, 1935).

Late 1930s: Philippines (Commonwealth),
Technical Committee to the President, *American-*
Philippine Trade Relations (Washington, D.C.:
n.p., 1944), table 87, p. 230.

a.   Includes investment in transportation.
b.   Includes export-processing industries, mining, and
agricultural and other real estate.
c.   Not including value of estimated ore reserves.
d.   For value of investment in transportation, see *United*
States-Philippines Trade.
e.   For value of investment, see *American-Philippine Trade*
Relations, table 44, p. 121.
nrs = not reported separately.

the export sector was attributable to the American decision
to devalue the dollar, which raised the price of gold to $35
an ounce, an increase of 70 percent. Stimulated by this
windfall, American investment in insular mining companies
increased more than fivefold during the 1930s.

American investment in public utilities, including
transportation facilities, accounted for a further
22 percent of American direct investment in the colony in
the late 1930s. The concentration of American investment in
export production and processing and public utilities at the
end of the colonial period was extreme, as these activities
accounted for more than four-fifths of all American direct
investment.

Although such investment conformed to tradition as it
moved into the export sector, development of the colony was
modest and the role of American investment limited compared
with other outlets for American capital competitive with the
Asian colony. For example, United States direct investment
of $919 million in Cuba in 1930 was virtually eight times
that in the Philippines, although the Philippine population
was three times that of Cuba and the land area two-and-a-
half times as great.[6]

When Congress drafted independence legislation in the
early 1930s, the Philippine economy was tightly integrated
with that of the United States by twenty-five years of
mutual free trade. The resulting Independence Act reflected
the conviction of Congress members generally that meaningful
independence for the new state must have an economic as well
as a political dimension, and that economic independence
required the dismantling of preferential trade. To begin
this process quotas were established on duty-free imports
from the colony of sugar, coconut oil, cordage, and a few
minor commodities to halt further specialization in
production of these products based on the protected American
market. Subject to these quotas, mutual free trade was

scheduled to continue for the first five years of the
autonomous Philippine Commonwealth, to be followed by five
years during which Philippine commodities would be subject
to gradually increasing export taxes, until in 1946, when
inauguration of the independent Philippine Republic was
scheduled, each commodity exported to the United States
would be paying a tax equal to 25 percent of the United
States tariff duty on the commodity. Congress also provided
for a joint Philippine-American Commission to plan the
postindependence transition during which remaining
preferences in mutual trade would be phased out. These
plans were interrupted by World War II and the subsequent
reinvolvement of the United States in the colony.

Almost without exception, Filipino political leaders
tenaciously resisted American determination to dismantle
preferential trade. At the same time, they insisted upon
another economic dimension of independence--the
Filipinization of the colonial-type economy in which alien
(Chinese) and foreign participation was prominent.
Insistence upon attainment of this goal characterized
Filipino participation in the insular legislature throughout
the American period and was affirmed by the convention
convened in 1934 to write the constitution for the
transitional Commonwealth government provided in the
Independence Act. The resulting constitution specified that
only Filipinos or enterprises at least 60 percent owned by
Filipinos could "exploit, develop, and use Philippine
natural resources including agricultural land" or "operate
public utilities." Subsequently, the Mining Act of 1936
restored the Hispanic "regalian doctrine," which vested the
ownership of all mineral resources in the national
government and provided for access to mineral resources by
lease contracts of specified duration. That year also saw
enactment of the Land Act of 1936, which extended the
nationality requirement for land ownership in the Philippine
Constitution to transfers of privately owned agricultural

137

land and reiterated the long-standing limit on the amount of land a corporation could own. These new measures left property rights established prior to their enactment undisturbed.[7]

With independence imminent, Congress, confronted by the complex task of tying off loose ends left from American reinvolvement in the Philippines during World War II, enacted two major pieces of economic legislation in 1946. The Philippine Rehabilitation Act provided for war-damage payments in excess of $600 million to assist in the rehabilitation of the island economy, which suffered grievously from the Japanese invasion and destruction attending liberation. The second law, the Bell Trade Act of 1946, established a new schedule for dismantling preferential trade and spread it over the twenty-eight years ending in 1974. The trade measure also included provisions infringing on the sovereignty of the new Republic of the Philippines, including the odious "parity amendment." The latter required the Filipinos to amend their constitution to establish national treatment for Americans and their enterprises in the exploitation of Philippine natural resources and operation of public utilities. Congress also specified that compensation for war damage would be contingent upon implementation by the Filipino society of the "parity" clause of the Bell Trade Act. This was done resentfully and under duress occasioned by the confusion, fears, and uncertainties confronting the new republic at the end of the war.[8]

The first five years of Philippine independence was a period in which the United States participated extensively in rehabilitation of the island economy. Including war damage payments, United States government expenditures under a range of programs totaled some $1.5 billion and sustained an import surplus in excess of $1 billion. The influx of goods and services provided the material requirements of

rapid rehabilitation and also played an essential role in
reestablishing internal monetary stability. Moreover, the
Bell Trade Act continued mutual free trade, and access to
the American market supported steady recovery of traditional
Philippine export industries. Investment incentives
remained concentrated in the export sector, however, as
mutual free trade and the flood of imports precluded
substantial manufacturing development based on the internal
market. Under these circumstances rehabilitation was
essentially a process of reconstructing the prewar colonial-
type economy, a process disappointing to Filipinos concerned
for the independence and sovereignty of their country and
the challenge to escape dependence on preferential access to
the United States market.

As the period of rehabilitation drew to a close,
official United States expenditures contracted, and
management of the Philippine balance of payments became
difficult. Among other factors, this reflected the
agreement of the Filipino leadership in 1946 to the
restoration of the prewar exchange rate of P2 per dollar,
which grossly overvalued the peso and maintained a level of
demand for imports and other foreign exchange expenditures
far in excess of foreign exchange earnings.[9]

To solve this problem, a task that became imperative as
foreign exchange reserves drained away, the Philippine
government installed import and exchange controls at the end
of 1949 and applied them with such intensity in 1950 that
imports were limited to three-fifths of their volume a year
earlier.[10] It was not surprising, therefore, that peso
prices of imported commodities rose sharply as importers
disposed of curtailed supplies at prices the Philippine
market would bear. With the installation of stringent
import and exchange controls, the Philippines embarked upon
a prolonged process of industrialization through import
substitution. Despite continuous controversy and widespread

concern for the corruption and economic distortions attending discretionary controls over economic activities, this strategy has been maintained to the present, although techniques for its implementation have undergone extensive adaptation.

Once management of the balance of payments was assured, the exchange control authorities quickly discovered that by requiring Philippine nationality as a qualification for foreign exchange allocation they could Filipinize import trade and the wholesaling of imports. With this experience behind them it did not take the Filipino leaders long to recognize that protection established by higher peso prices of restricted imports and the windfall in foreign exchange allocated to import raw and semifinished materials could be used to maintain powerful incentives to manufacture in the Philippines commodities denied access to the Philippine market by import controls. The widespread enthusiasm generated by the initial industrialization based upon import substitution moderated concern for Filipinization, and foreign and alien enterprises sharing in the manufacturing incentives encountered relatively little overt discrimination.

Over the twelve years that the prewar peso exchange rate was maintained by controls and the import-substitution strategy was in full flower, the value added by manufacturing as a share of Philippine national income virtually doubled to 18 percent. This was also a period in which United States direct investment increased rapidly from $149 million in 1950 to $415 million at the end of 1961. As could be expected, the fastest-growing sector of United States direct investment was manufacturing, including petroleum refining, which increased to one-half of total direct investment as investment in this sector expanded ninefold from the level of $23 million recorded in 1950.[11]

By the late 1950s, it became evident that stresses and distortions in the system of exchange and import controls and corruption in their implementation were undermining the import-substitution strategy, and early in 1962 the peso was devalued to P3.90 per dollar, roughly half of the previous official rate. The effect of this decision was to redirect incentives to invest from the manufacturing sector to the export sector, and successive devaluations in 1970 and 1971, and steady deterioration in the peso's value thereafter, have maintained this priority. At the same time, growth in manufacturing for the domestic market has been sustained by conventional protection implemented by tariff duties in conjunction with subsidized credit and tax concessions. As a result, the contribution of export production to national income increased slowly, while the share of income generated by manufacturing remained relatively stable as economic growth of the Philippine economy averaged in excess of 5 percent annually over the 1960s and 1970s.

The preoccupation of Philippine policymakers with economic nationalism resumed with the installation of stringent import and exchange controls and has continued to the present. Laws extending nationality restrictions on access to shipping activities, domestic air transport, oil exploration and production, cooperatives, and the range of financial institutions, including commercial banks, accumulated steadily during the autonomous Commonwealth and following independence. The success with which exchange controls were used to Filipinize the import trade could not be duplicated in retail trade or trade in rice and corn in which Chinese participation was prominent. Frustrated by the lack of progress in these areas, the Philippine Congress formally Filipinized these activities in the 1950s by legislation limiting them to wholly owned Filipino firms.[12]

Goals of economic nationalism were also pursued through administrative discretion vested in major regulatory bodies.

141

For example, the Monetary Board implemented regulations which raised the required ratio of Filipino participation in new commercial banks to levels well above the 60 percent prescribed in the Banking Act of 1948. In 1959 the board announced that establishment of new branches of existing commercial banks would require prior approval of the board, and it used this action to delay for years proposals by the two American banks in the Philippines to open branches in the burgeoning Makati financial district in suburban Manila.[13]

Similarly, the Public Service Commission sat on, and frequently rejected, applications for rate increases submitted by the Manila Electric Company and the Philippine Long Distance Telephone Company so long as they were American-owned. This behavior adversely affected the utility services provided and generated customer complaints and adverse publicity which undoubtedly contributed to the decision of the American owners to sell out to Filipinos. In the midst of the OPEC embargo in the fall of 1973, the Petroleum Commission was created to regulate petroleum refining and marketing. In carrying out this mandate it maintained pressure on foreign firms that dominated these activities, and recent years have seen transfers of major American-owned units to Filipino ownership.[14]

Philippine courts also helped to erect the policy structure of economic nationalism. Every law establishing nationality restrictions on participation in economic activities enacted since the proclamation of Philippine independence has been upheld by the courts. The courts have not been laggard in providing initiative on their own. For example, the Supreme Court applied in the Krivenko decision (1947) the constitutional requirement that "exploitation" of natural resources be limited to Filipinos, and decreed that non-Filipinos could not establish legal title to land. The court concluded that all land in private ownership was "agricultural land," on the ground that it had at one time been in the public domain and was initially alienated for agricultural purposes (i.e., "exploitation") which the constitution limits to Filipinos and to enterprises at least 60 percent Filipino-owned. As the end of the transition to nonpreferential trade approached, the Supreme Court established in the Quasha case the principle that property rights established under the "parity amendment" to the constitution would terminate with the end of preferential trade. This decision forced the divestment of major American interests in Philippine natural-resource industries in recent years.[15]

Last but not least, in drafting the Investment Incentives Act of 1967, the Philippine Congress sharply curtailed access by foreigners and aliens to manufacturing activities, which remained relatively open to non-Filipinos during the early period of industrialization via import substitution. In doing so, Congress created a Board of Investments to regulate investment in accordance with an annual "investment priorities plan." A variety of incentives were provided to encourage new enterprises and the law is permeated with complex provisions, the interpretation of which is left to the Board of Investments, which ensures that Filipinos will be favored in access to investment incentives.[16]

The invitation to the non-Filipino investor proves less than wholehearted, however, as a non-Filipino firm qualifying for incentives under the law as a "preferred" or "pioneer" activity must begin promptly to transform itself into a Filipino enterprise. Such enterprises are obligated to begin selling out to Filipinos not later than twenty years following approval by the Board of Investments of its proposal to operate in the Philippines, and the proportion of Filipino ownership must reach at least 60 percent within thirty years.

143

Given this brief survey of Philippine foreign-investment policy during the American period and since independence, what is the stake of American capital and enterprise in the Philippines at present, and how has this economic presence changed in recent years? The surge of United States direct investment stimulated by the incentives in the import-substitution strategy was drastically slowed by devaluation of the peso in 1962 and the growing militancy of Philippine economic nationalism. Subsequently, articulation of Filipino resentment of the "parity amendment" became shrill as the end of preferential trade approached. The resulting uncertainty concerning the future of property rights established by Americans under "parity" inhibited the movement of American capital and enterprise to the Philippines and encouraged the repatriation of American direct investment in parity sectors.

Official American recognition of the futility of "parity" as a device with which to maintain national treatment for American enterprises was acknowledged by the Johnson administration in the mid-1960s. On different occasions President Johnson, Assistant Secretary of State William Bundy, and Ambassador G. Mennan Williams assured Filipinos that the United States would not seek renewal of parity when preferential trade ceased in 1974.[17] Shortly thereafter, enactment of the Investment Incentives Act imposed conditions which could only curtail the interest of potential American investors in manufacturing for the local market, the sector which sustained rapid growth of American direct investment in the Philippines following 1950.

The impact of these factors is reflected in the rate of growth in United States direct investment in the 1960s and the interruption of growth as the trade transition drew to a close. During the decade of the 1950s, United States direct investment in the Philippines increased from $149 million to $414 million, and the ratio of American direct investment in

GOLAY

TABLE 2

United States Direct Investment,
Global and in the Philippines, 1950-1977
(U.S. $million, end of year)

	Total $ billion	Index 1960=100	Philippines ($ million)	Index 1960=100	Share of Philippines (percent)
1950	11.8	36	149	36	1.26
1957	24.4	77	183	44	.77
1960	32.8	100	414	100	1.26
1963	40.7	124	415	100	1.02
1966	54.7	167	579	140	1.06
1969	71.0	216	742	179	1.04
1972	94.3	288	608	147	.64
1975	133.2	406	738	178	.55
1976	136.4	416	831	201	.61
1977	149.8	457	913	221	.61

Source: U.S. Department of Commerce, *Survey of Current Business*, various issues presenting annual survey of U.S. direct investment.

the Philippines to global direct investment of the United States at the end of 1960 (1.26 percent) was unchanged from that of a decade earlier (see table 2). The rate of growth in United States direct investment slowed in the 1960s, but such investment continued to grow until it peaked at $742 million in 1969. Over the following six years, through 1975, there was no growth in United States direct investment in the Philippines and the Philippine share of American global direct investment sagged to .55 percent, less than half the Philippine share fifteen years earlier. Thereafter, United States direct investment exceeded the level reached in 1969; at the end of 1977 it amounted to

$913 million, six-tenths of one percent of American global
direct investment.

During the twenty-eight years ending in 1977, the rate
of growth in United States direct investment drastically
slowed. Over the decade of the 1950s, American direct
investment grew by 177 percent. In the decade of the 1960s,
the rate of increase fell to 69 percent and during the first
eight years of the 1970s the increase was only 30 percent
(see table 3). The period analyzed, moreover, was one of
stability followed by increasing inflation, particularly in
the 1970s. When United States direct investment is deflated
for price changes, the decline in the rate of growth becomes
more drastic. Using the increase in the decade of the 1950s
as the base, the increase in United States direct investment
in the 1960s fell to 71 percent of the previous decade, and
the increase over the eight years ending in 1977 was only
14 percent of the rate of investment in the 1950s.

II

Analysis of the composition and recent changes in
United States direct investment in the Philippines is
facilitated by a detailed survey of the 169 largest American
direct-investment enterprises in the Philippines in 1970,
compiled from accounting statements these corporations are
required to file with the Philippine Securities and Exchange
Commission. This survey, which is summarized in appendix A,
includes information on the United States ownership share
and net worth of the enterprises, which permits the value of
American-owned equity to be established for each firm.

The value of the United States ownership share in the
169 firms surveyed in 1970 totaled P2,667 million (see table
4). When converted at the peso/dollar exchange rate for
1970, American investment in these firms amounted to
$684 million. The aggregate value of American-owned equity
in these firms was equal to 96 percent of total American

146

TABLE 3

United States Direct Investment in the Philippines,
1950–1977
(U.S. $million, end of year)

| | | Current Value | | | Value in constant 1972 prices | |
	Total	Increase in value over period	Rate of increase in value	Increase in value over period[a]	Index of increase in value over period (1950–60=100)
1950	149				
1960	414				
(1950–1960)		265	177%	669	100
1970	701				
(1960–1970)		287	69%	474	71
1977	913				
(1970–1977)		212	30%	91	14

Source: U.S. Department of Commerce, *Survey of Current Business*, various issues presenting annual survey of U.S. direct investment.

a. Sum of annual increases in U.S. direct investment, in current dollars, deflated by implicit price index (1972=100) for Philippine gross domestic capital-formation. See R.P., National Economic and Development Authority (NEDA), *Philippine Statistical Yearbook, 1978* (Manila: NEDA, 1979), 154–59, table 4.8.

TABLE 4

Distribution of United States Ownership of Net Worth
by Industrial Category for the 169 Largest United States
Direct-Investment Enterprises in the Philippines in 1970

	P million	Percent of total
Natural resource exploitation (12)	475.0	17.7
Export processors (20)	184.8	6.9
Manufacturing for domestic market (73)	1057.7	39.7
Commerce (44)	571.1	21.4
Service enterprises (14)	137.5	5.2
Public utilities (3)	4.9	.2
Insurance and banking (4)	235.5	8.8
Total (169)[a]	2,666.5	99.9[b]

Source: See appendix A.

a. Number of firms totals 169 because U.S.-owned net worth
in Caltex was divided equally between "Manufacturing
for the domestic market" and "Commerce."

b. Percentages do not total 100.0 due to rounding.

direct investment in the Philippines as reported by the
United States Department of Commerce for 1970. The
remainder of American direct investment in 1970 was
accounted for by direct-investment firms too small to be
included in the survey.[18]

Of the 169 United States direct-investment firms
surveyed, those engaged in manufacturing for the domestic
market accounted for two-fifths of aggregate American
ownership of the firms surveyed. Enterprises engaged in

148

commerce (export/import and internal distribution) accounted for a further 21 percent of the value of American ownership of the 169 firms. The relative importance of United States direct investment in manufacturing for the Philippine market in 1970 contrasts sharply with American participation in this sector in the late colonial period when the value of United States direct investment in manufacturing ranged from one-sixteenth to one-twentieth of total direct investment.

Natural resource industries accounted for P475 million of United States ownership in the firms covered by the 1970 survey, or 18 percent of total United States ownership, and the American share of firms engaged in processing exports added another 7 percent. American ownership of direct-investment firms operating public utilities in 1970 amounted to P5 million, or one-fifth of one percent of all United States investment in the firms surveyed. This small share is surprising in view of the national treatment extended to American capital and enterprise in this sector by the "parity amendment" and the attractiveness of this sector to American investors in the late colonial period, when investment in utilities accounted for one-quarter to one-fifth of all United States direct investment. The remainder of the United States ownership share of the 169 firms surveyed was employed in service enterprises and insurance and banking, which accounted for P373 million, or 14 percent of total American ownership.

United States direct investment in 1970 was heavily concentrated in a few firms. The American ownership share of the five firms with the largest American-owned net worth totaled P952 million or 38 percent of all United States direct investment in that year; the ten largest firms accounted for P1,318 million, or 53 percent, and the firms with the twenty largest American-ownership shares accounted for P1,713 million, more than two-thirds of all United States direct investment in 1970 (see table 5). Equally

distinctive is the high proportion of American ownership in
United States direct-investment enterprises in the
Philippines in 1970. The forty largest firms included
twenty-three that were wholly American-owned plus five
others with American ownership ranging from 90 to
99 percent. Only one firm reported less than 50 percent
American ownership (see appendix B).

TABLE 5

Concentration in American Ownership of
United States Direct-Investment
Enterprises in the Philippines in 1970

Number of enterprises	U.S. ownership of net worth	
	P million	Percent of total for nonfinancial enterprises
Five largest	952	38
Ten largest	1,318	53
Twenty largest	1,713	69
Forty largest	2,057	82
One hundred and sixty-four largest	2,431	97
All nonfinancial firms	2,498	100
Four financial enterprises	236	
Total, all direct-investment enterprises	2,734[a]	

Source: See appendix B.

a. Total United States direct investment in the Philippines
in 1970, reported by the U.S. Department of Commerce,
converted to pesos at the rate of P3.90 per dollar.

Similarly, American ownership of United States direct-investment firms was highly concentrated in a few activities. In 1970 the three United States direct-investment enterprises in petroleum refining and the three largest United States direct-investment enterprises in petroleum distribution included American ownership shares totaling P631 million, or 25 percent of all nonfinancial United States direct investment in the enterprises surveyed (see appendix A). The three American firms in mining included American ownership totaling P397 million, or 16 percent of United States direct investment in the firms surveyed. Three American enterprises engaged in the manufacture of automotive tires accounted for a further 6 percent of United States direct investment in 1970.

The gradual intensification of the pressures of Philippine nationalism on Americans and their enterprises induced steady disinvestment by Americans following 1960, a process that peaked sharply in 1973, the final year of the Laurel-Langley transition to nonpreferential trade. Administrative discretion vested in the Philippine Public Service Commission was used to deny applications for rate increases from American-owned utility enterprises, and 1967 saw the transfer to Filipino ownership of the Philippine Long Distance Telephone Company, the last American-owned utility enterprise of any size. Similarly, the series of court decisions culminating in the decision that property rights obtained under the "parity" clause were not vested but would expire in mid-1974 initiated an exodus of capital from enterprises exploiting natural resources (see table 6). In some cases, for example, Atlas Consolidated, Lepanto Mining, and Philrock, sufficient equity was transferred to Filipinos to comply with the national requirement of the Philippine Constitution. In others, for example, Insular Lumber Company, the American owners decided to take their capital and go home.

TABLE 6

Disinvestment by United States Nonfinancial Direct-
Investment Firms in the Philippines, 1962-1972

	$ million	P million
Manila Electric (1962). Sale of U.S. equity share of 100% to Filipinos.	46.9	
Atlas Consolidated (1966). Announced intention to increase Filipino ownership share between 1966 and end of 1970. Filipino ownership share increased from 9% to 41%.	55.0	
Lepanto Mining (1967). Sale of U.S. equity equivalent to 40%, increasing Filipino equity to 65%.	6.0	
Philippine Long Distance Telephone Co. (1967). Sale of U.S. equity equivalent to 28%. Filipine ownership share increased to 60% plus.	14.8	
Luzon Stevedoring (1972). Sale of 86% of U.S. equity.		96.0[a]
Philrock (1968). Sale of 60% of U.S. equity. Further sale in 1970 of additional 10% of U.S. equity.	7.0	
Philippine Airlines (1968). Equity share of 20% held by Pan Am sold to Filipinos.	4.0	
Manila Trading Co. (1968). Sale of U.S. equity share of 100% to Filipinos.	4.0	
Atlantic, Gulf & Pacific (1970). Sale of U.S. equity share of 60% to Filipinos. Commitment to transfer additional U.S. equity share of 37%.	3.0[a]	27.2[a]
Esso Standard Fertilizer (1970). Sale of U.S. equity share to Filipinos. Ratio of U.S. equity transferred not indicated.		209.3[a]
Maria Christina Chemicals (1970). Sale of U.S. equity share of 50% to Filipinos.	.9	

	$ million	P million
Luzon Brokerage (1970). Sale of U.S. equity to Filipinos.	.6	
Norton and Harrison (1968). Sale of U.S.-owned equity share of 100% to Filipinos.	.5	
Philippine Oil Development Co. (1970). Sale of U.S. equity share of 25% to Filipinos. Filipino ownership share increased to 61%.	.6	
Insular Lumber Co. (1971). Sale of U.S. share of equity 97% to Filipinos.		13.8[a]
A. Soriano y Cia. (1972). Announcement that 60% of equity would be sold to Filipinos, of which 40% to 45% would be offered to Filipino employees in the Soriano group of companies.		55.0[b]
Totals	143.3	401.3
Total in U.S. dollar equivalent	$246.2[c]	

Source: American Chamber of Commerce (Manila), *Memorandum Listing Actual Past U.S. Disinvestments in the Philippines*, 18 December, 1970.

a. L. S. Coates, "American Disinvestment in the Philippines, January 1970-September 1972, 22 December 1972," research paper prepared for Asian Studies 501A, fall term, 1972, Cornell University.

b. Sixty percent of equity as of 1970. A. Soriano Y Cia was entirely U.S.-owned in 1970.

c. Philippine pesos converted to U.S. dollars at P3.90 per dollar.

Divestments unrelated to "parity" also occurred. The American owners of Esso Standard Fertilizer, Manila Trading Company, Atlantic, Gulf and Pacific Company, and Luzon Brokerage Company decided to sell out to Filipinos. Over the eleven years ending with 1972, transfers of American-owned equity to Filipinos totaled not less than $246 million.

The magnitude of divestment of American-owned equity since 1960 also reflects the policy of the Philippine government to facilitate the transfer of foreign-owned firms to Filipinos. We can assume that Filipino purchasers acquired profitable enterprises, and, so long as their government stood ready to convert the peso earnings of such enterprises to the dollars needed to pay for the equity acquired, their acquisition by Filipinos was relatively painless.

In 1973 the rate of disinvestment jumped sharply when transfers equivalent to $80 million were announced in the press (see table 7). Because of exchange-rate changes over the period covered, as well as internal inflation in the Philippines and the lag in time over which the accounting value of business assets is adjusted to reflect increases in replacement cost of plant and equipment and the value of inventories, attempts to value disinvestment taking place over a span of years in dollars of constant value can only be impressionistic. It seems clear, however, that in current prices some $327 million of United States direct investment was divested over the thirteen years following 1960.

Also of interest is the impact of this process of divestment upon the relative importance of American participation in various industries. The sale of 60 percent of the equity in Benguet Consolidated in conjunction with previously existing Filipino-owned equity in this major gold producer eliminated United States direct investment in gold

TABLE 7

Disinvestment by United States Nonfinancial Direct-
Investment Firms in the Philippines, 1973-1974

	P million
Benguet Consolidated (*Manila Daily Bulletin*, 11/23/73). Announcement of sale of U.S. equity equivalent to 60% of total equity for P202.5 million. Hereafter the *Manila Daily Bulletin* will be listed as *Bulletin*.	202.5
Esso Philippines and Bataan Refining (*Bulletin*, 12/22/73). Announcement of sale of 100% of Esso Philippines and Esso's 53% ownership of Bataan Refining to Philippine government for $19.5 million.	130.7
Atlas Consolidated (*Bulletin*, 10/27/73). Announcement that Filipino onwership had reached 61%.	52.2[a]
Theo H. Davis (*Business Day*, 10/1/73). Announcement of sale of U.S. interest to Jardine-Matheson, a Hong Kong firm.	32.9
Filoil Refining (*Bulletin*, 8/7/73). Announcement of sale of Gulf Oil equity to Philippine government.	28.4[b]
Marcopper (*Bulletin*, 10/27/73). Announcement of plans to complete transfer of remaining U.S. equity to Filipinos, increasing Filipino ownership share to 60%.	47.5[b]
Bislig Bay Lumber Co. (*Business Day*, 10/31/73). Absorbed into Paper Industry Corporation of the Philippines (PCIOP). It is assumed that this firm will comply with the constitutional requirement of 60% Filipino ownership.	10.2[c]
Legaspi Oil (*Bulletin*, 11/13/73). Announcement that Ayala interest would acquire U.S.-owned equity equal to 60% of total.	9.8
Manila Cordage (*Bulletin*, 11/26/73). Announcement of sale of U.S. equity to Filipinos.	9.2
Rheem of the Philippines (*Business Day*, 11/7/73). Announcement that A. Soriano Corp. had purchased the American-owned equity of Rheem International.	4.3[d]

	P million
Engineering Equipment, Inc. (*Business Day*, 12/13/73). Public offering of shares to Filipinos.	3.9
Warner Barnes (*Bulletin*, 8/22/73). Enterprise is referred to as "now a Filipino-owned firm."	2.8
Paracale Gumaus Mining Co. (*Bulletin*, 10/26/73). Inactive U.S.-owned mining company sold to Philippine consortium.	2.8
Mahogany Products (Phils.), Inc. (*Bulletin*, 2/19/74). Reports of sale in 1973 to a Filipino.	<u>2.1</u>
Total	P539.3

a. As of 1970, the U.S. ownership share was 54 percent and Filipino share 41 percent. It is assumed that the increase in the Filipino ownership share to 61 percent resulted from the transfer of equity from U.S. to Filipino ownership. Estimated equity transferred is 20 percent of equity as of 1970.

b. Value of U.S. ownership share in 1970.

c. As of 1970, the U.S. ownership share was 56 percent. It is assumed that the Filipino ownership share was 44 percent in 1970 and that the increase in the Filipino ownership share to 60 percent resulted from the transfer of 16 percent of equity from the U.S. ownership share to Filipinos.

d. Amount indicated is 60 percent of equity in 1970.

mining. With the sale of American-owned net worth in Marcopper and the reduction of American ownership in Atlas Consolidated to 40 percent, the latter is the only significant United States direct investment left in Philippine mining.

Although data available to the author are not complete, it is clear that disinvestment of United States direct investment in forestry industries has been substantial. American direct-investment firms remaining in the manufacture of lumber and plywood are either buying their

logs from Filipino enterprises or have reduced the United
States equity share as necessary to comply with the
nationality requirement of the Philippine Constitution.

Still another interesting divestment is that of
Theo H. Davies Company, which wiped out the last significant
United States direct investments in the sugar industry, as
this firm was the holding company and manager for Hawaiian-
Philippines, San Carlos, and Bogo-Medellen, the only
remaining United States direct-investment sugar mills.

One crucial question remains to be considered. What is
the relative importance of American direct investment in the
Philippine economy? Fortunately for this study, the
Philippine National Economic and Development Authority
(NEDA) publishes a compilation of historical social accounts
for the Philippines, valued both in current and 1972 prices.
These data permit a relatively reliable estimate of the
ratio of total American direct investment to the value of
the capital stock of the Philippines at the end of 1977.
Using the assumption that the ratio of capital to output has
remained stable over time, and valuing incremental capital
and output in constant 1972 prices, results in the
conclusion that American direct investment was equal to
2.6 percent of the capital stock of the Philippines at the
end of 1977 (see table 8). It would be farfetched to
conclude from this evidence that American capital and
enterprise dominated the Philippine economy as the decade of
the 1970s drew to a close.[19]

Other data lend credence to the conclusion that
American capital and enterprise have played a steadily
contracting role in the Philippine economy over the past two
decades. For example, at the end of 1977 the value of
American direct investment, converted to pesos at the
average exchange rate for 1977, was equivalent to
8.1 percent of the assets of the one thousand largest
Philippine corporations.[20] If the value of the assets of

GOLAY

TABLE 8

Estimate of Philippine Capital Stock in 1977 and
the Ratio of United States Direct Investment in 1977
to Philippine Capital Stock
(P billion, constant 1972 prices)

National income, 1977	63.0
National income, 1968	38.6
Increase in national income, 1968-77	24.4
Net domestic capital formation, 1968-77[a]	88.8
Average capital/output ratio, 1968-77	3.64
Estimated Philippine capital stock, 1977[b]	229.3
U.S. direct investment, 1977[c]	6.059
Ratio of U.S direct investment to Philippine capital stock, 1977	2.6%

Source: R.P., NEDA, *Philippine Statistical Yearbook, 1978*,
162-63, table 4.10 (Net national product or
national income and capital consumption
allowance); and 152-53, table 4.7 (Gross domestic
capital formation).

a. Sum of annual, gross, domestic capital-formation,
1968-1977, less sum of annual capital-consumption
allowances, 1968-1977.

b. Capital stock (1977) = National income (1977)
multiplied by average capital-output ratio (1968-1977).

c. U.S. direct investment, 1977, converted to pesos at
average dollar exchange-rate used in valuing Philippine
trade in 1972. R.P., Bureau of Census and Statistics,
Foreign Trade Statistics of the Philippines, 1972
(Manila: Bureau of Census and Statistics, 1973), X.

158

TABLE 9

Distribution of Commercial Bank Credit in the
Philippines by Nationality of Borrower

	Credits granted 1/1/1960 to 9/30/1974		Loans outstanding (percent of total)	
	P billion	percent of total	12/31/1960	12/31/1979
Filipino	220.5	81.6	74.7	92.8
American	19.5	7.2	11.0	4.3
Other	30.2	11.2	24.3	2.9

Source: *Statistical Bulletin, 1977* (Manila: Central
         Bank of the Philippines, 1978), 55, table 19,
         and 65, table 24; *Statistical Bulletin, 1978*
         (Manila: Central Bank of the Philippines, 1979),
         65, table 24.

the remaining Philippine corporations, plus those of
proprietorships, partnerships, and farm enterprises, were
taken into account, it is unlikely that the ratio of the
value of American direct investment to the value of all
assets of nongovernmental enterprises at the end of 1977 was
as much as 4 percent.

Another measure of the change in the relative
importance of the role played by American direct investment
following 1960 is the change in the share of credit extended
and loans outstanding going to Americans and their
enterprises. Over the period beginning with 1960 and ending
September 30, 1974, credits granted by Philippine commercial
banks totaled P270 billion, of which P220.5 billion was
extended to Filipinos and P19.5 billion, or 7.2 percent,
went to Americans and their enterprises (see table 9). This
measure must be used with caution, however, as a reliable
measure of the use of available credit must include a time

factor proportionate to the time the credit was available to the borrower as well as the amount of the credit extended. For example, one firm may borrow ₱1,000 for thirty days and renew that loan each month for twelve months, while another firm may borrow ₱1,000 for twelve months. Credit extended to the first borrower would total ₱12,000, while that to the second borrower would be listed as ₱1,000, although each borrower had the use of ₱1,000 of credit for twelve months. That access of Americans and their enterprises to Philippine commercial bank credit is overstated by data on total credit granted is confirmed by data on commercial bank credit outstanding. At the end of 1960, credits outstanding to Americans and their enterprises totaled ₱119.7, or 11.0 percent of credits outstanding. At the end of 1977, the American share was down to 4.3 percent (see table 9).

The opportunities to acquire land in the Philippines never excited American interest, and agricultural land owned by Americans at the end of 1938 totaled 171,330 hectares, or 2 percent of all land in private hands. As the transition to nonpreferential trade was drawing to a close in the early 1970s, the United States Embassy reported that Americans and their enterprises owned 17,300 hectares of land. American ownership of land amounted, therefore, to one-fifth of one percent of the area in farms, totaling 8,494,000 hectares.[21]

When confronted with these data, Filipinos frequently dismiss them as irrelevant in assessing the relative importance of American capital and enterprise in the agricultural sector, citing arrangements made by Philippine Packing Company and Dole Philippines, Inc., to grow commercial crops on land leased from the government. The lease of the Philippine Packing Company (8,195 hectares of public agricultural land) was renewed for twenty-five years by the National Development Company in 1963. In the same year the National Development Company entered into an agreement with Dole Philippines, Inc., in which the National

Development Company agreed to acquire land to be made
available to Dole on a twenty-five-year lease to grow
pineapples and other agricultural crops. As of 1964 the
lands leased to Dole under the agreement totaled 3,529
hectares. The 11,724 hectares of land leased to American
direct-investment enterprises was equal to slightly more
than one-third of one percent of the area harvested to
Philippine commercial crops in 1976. Land owned or leased
by Americans and their enterprises in the 1970s totaled some
29,000 hectares, or one-third of one percent of all
Philippine agricultural lands in private hands.[22]

American ownership of Philippine land acquired prior to
enactment of the Bell Trade Act in 1946 will contract
steadily in the future, as title to these lands can be
transferred only to direct heirs of their American owners,
to Filipinos, or to enterprises with not less than
60 percent Filipino ownership.

In 1974 the Philippine Supreme Court, in the Quasha
case, scheduled the termination of titles to land acquired
by American corporations after the proclamation of
Philippine independence in 1946. In response to this
situation, the Marcos government initially announced that a
government corporation would be created to take title to
lands acquired by Americans following 1946, some seven
thousand hectares, under escheat proceedings decreed by the
government.[23]

Meanwhile, martial law was declared and the Marcos
government--aware of the accelerating exodus of American
direct investment--proved to be uninterested in using the
Quasha decision to hasten that exodus. On May 27, 1974, a
presidential proclamation was issued declaring that parity
rights acquired by Americans would be resolved upon
termination of the transition to nonpreferential trade and
that no action would be taken meanwhile to "alter the
present situation." A day later, Presidential Decree 471

was issued, permitting American corporations to continue to
occupy land under a lease limited to twenty-five years,
renewable for a second twenty-five years.[24]

Marcos's proclamation and decree were followed by a
series of land-divestment proposals by American corporations
which would allow them to continue to use the land they
occupied. Although the various proposals differed in
detail, they all involved the transfer of title to American-
owned land to a Filipino realty company, a Filipino
charitable institution, or the pension fund of the Filipino
employees of the American corporation, in conjunction with a
lease-back arrangement permitting the corporation to use the
land, subject to the lease duration permitted by
Presidential Decree 471.

Finally, Filipinos believe that American direct
investment is a source of a large and growing drain on
Philippine foreign-exchange earnings. During the seventeen
years ending with 1976, global remittances of direct-
investment income from the Philippines increased from an
average of $45 million in 1960-62 to an average of
$74 million in 1974-76, an increase of two-thirds (see table
10). Over the periods compared, average remittances of
direct-investment income fell from 8.3 percent of export
earnings in 1960-62 to 3.0 percent in 1974-76. Other
investment income remitted, primarily interest paid on
loans, increased 45-fold, from an average of $5 million to
$227 million annually over the periods compared. At the
same time, investment income received by the Philippines
from abroad increased 22-fold, from an average of $7 million
to $156 million annually. By 1974-76, investment income
received by the Philippines from abroad was more than double
the global direct-investment income remitted from the
Philippines. When account is taken of the decrease in the
value of the dollar since 1960, it is clear that the real

value of global remittances of direct-investment income has
declined over this period.

TABLE 10

Investment Income Account in the Philippines
Balance of Payments, 1960-1976
(annual average, U.S. $million)

	Investment Income Remitted			Investment income received	Net remittance of investment income
	Direct investment	Other	Total		
1960-62	45	5	50	7	43
1967-69	60	36	96	9	87
1974-76	74	227	301	156	145

Source: *Philippine Statistical Yearbook, 1978*, 490-91,
table 12.1.

III

Substantial numbers of educated and sophisticated
Filipinos of various persuasions choose to believe that
their economy is dominated by American-owned enterprises and
that they live in thralldom to American direct-investment
enterprises--the so-called multinational corporations. To
do so, these Filipinos reject a broad spectrum of objective
evidence to the contrary, major elements of which are
summarized above.

Explanations of this pattern of Filipino behavior vary.
We can readily understand why Filipino businessmen cling to
this belief, because they have been the principal
beneficiaries of policies of economic nationalism which
restricted the competition of foreign- and alien-owned

163

enterprises. Moreover, to the extent that non-Filipino entrepreneurs respond to the pressures of Philippine economic nationalism by deciding to disinvest, Filipino businessmen will continue to acquire profitable enterprises at favorable prices.

Other Filipinos--many of whom are found in the bureaucracy--march to the militant rhetoric of the "Group of 77," projecting the image of a world polarized into a poor South exploited by an affluent North. Taking this position offers the prospect of material benefits so long as the South remains militant and united. To do so also promises to improve the credibility of Filipino nationalism heretofore suspect in the Third World.

Then there are Filipinos who are disturbed by the disappearance of the open political system they took for granted and the mounting evidence of the durability of the authoritarian structure which replaced it. Frustrated by their inability to rectify the situation in which they find themselves, many of these Filipinos succumb to anthropomorphic escapism which assuages their consciences by placing the blame for their condition on the shoulders of others.

Appendix A

United States-Owned Net Worth by Major Categories
for the 169 Largest United States Direct-Investment
Enterprises in the Philippines in 1970 (Firms listed in
parentheses in order of value of U.S.-owned net worth)

	Number of firms	U.S. owned net worth (P million)
Natural resource exploitation		
Mining (Atlas Consolidated, Marcopper, Benguet Consolidated)	3	397.0
Logging, lumber, plywood, veneer (Bislig Bay, Zamboanga Wood Prods., Weyerhaeuser, Insular Lumber, Phil.-American Timber,* Mahogany Prods., Heald Lumber,* Johnston Lumber,* Findlay-Millar)	9	78.0
	12	475.0
Export processors		
Fruit growers and processors (Phil. Packing, Dole, Standard Fruit)	3	83.6
Sugar mills (Hawaiian-Phil., San Carlos, Bogo Medellin)	3	45.9
Coconut oil mills (Legaspi Oil, San Pablo)	2	18.7
Coconut products (Franklin Baker, Matalin)	2	9.1
Cordage (Manila Cordage)	1	9.2

	Number of firms	U.S. owned net worth (P million)
Exporters and consigners of embroideries, gloves, handicrafts, etc. (Gelmart, Novelty, Orion, Royal Undergarment, Phil. Handicrafts, Judy Phils.,* Phil. Gloves,* Supreme Baby Wear,* South Seas Trading*)	9	18.3
	20	184.8
Manufacturing for domestic market		
Petroleum refining (Bataan Refining, Caltex,[a] Filoil)	3	295.2
Automotive tires (Goodrich, Firestone, Goodyear)	3	147.2
Chemicals, paints, photographic materials, compressed gases, etc. (Union Carbide, Borden, Kodak, Fuller Paint, National Lead, S.C. Johnson, Phil. Acetylene, Cyanamid, Amfil,* Columbian Carbon, Sherwin-Williams,* Phil. Chemical Laboratory,* Phil. Rubber Project*)	13	85.0
Pharmaceutical and infants' nutritional products (Pfizer; Mead Johnson; Johnson & Johnson; Winthrop-Stearns; Warner-Chilcott; Richardson-Merrell; Abbott; Wyeth-Suaco; Squibb; Parke Davis; Merck, Sharp & Dohme; Upjohn; Eli Lilly; Estraco; Rachelle;* Robins;* Smith, Kline & French;* Bristol;* Rexall*)	19	77.4
Soft drinks and syrups (Pepsi Cola Bottling, Pepsi Cola F.E. Trade Dev., Coca Cola Export, SPT Extract*)	4	70.9
Toiletries, detergents, etc. (Proctor and Gamble,[b] Colgate-Palmolive)	2	67.0
Metals fabrication and engineering (Honiron Phils., Reynolds Phils., Rheem, Chicago Bridge, American Machinery and Parts*)	5	66.5

	Number of firms	U.S. owned net worth (P million)
Machinery and transport equipment (International Harvester-Macleod, Ford, Chrysler)	3	66.1
Other industrial products (American Wire and Cable, Republic Glass, Phelps Dodge)	3	52.4
Electrical and electronic appliances and apparatus (General Electric, Aircon, General Telephone and Electronics, Phil. Appliance, Phil. Electrical Mfg.)	5	39.1
Reconstituted milk (General Milk, Consolidated)	2	30.1
Food processing and related products (California Mfg., Wrigley, Far East Corn Refining, Standard Brands*)	4	26.3
Paper and related products (Scott Paper, Kimberly Clark, Phil. Paper Products*)	3	17.7
Sewing machines (Singer Industries, Singer Sewing Machine)	1	12.8
Other manufacturing enterprises (Muller & Phipps)	2	4.0
	73	1,057.7

Commerce, importing, exporting, distribution in domestic market

	Number of firms	U.S. owned net worth (P million)
Gasoline and automotive products (Mobil, Caltex,[a] Esso, Getty)	4	354.1
Machinery and equipment (USIPHIL, Edward J. Nell, Edward R. Bacon, Gould Pumps,* Shurdut Industrial Distributors,* Liberty Aviation,* Otis Elevator,* Ingersoll Rand,* Mastadon Equip.*)	9	72.5
Specialized importers and distributors (Phils. Remnants, Ault & Wiborg, Minnesota Mining and Mfg. (3M), P.F. Collier, Oceanic Commercial, Grolier, B.B. Fischer,* Solex Tool,* Newsweek,* J.P. Heilbronn*)	10	60.0

	Number of firms	U.S. owned net worth (P million)
Office machinery, equipment, and parts (IBM Phils., Burroughs, NCR,c Taylor Pacific)	4	36.7
General importing, wholesaling, brokerage (Muller & Phipps, Macondray, Connel Bros., Warner Barnes, Atkins Kroll, Williams Equip.*)	6	29.2
Pharmaceuticals and related products (Sterling Prods., Ayerst Labs., Inhelder-Don Baxter, Inhelder Corp., Shering)	5	9.6
Primarily exporters (Granexport, Lancaster Phils., Bunning & Co., Conrad & Co.*)	4	5.2
Other firms classified under "Commerce" (Luneta Motors,* Lawyers Coop. Publishing*)	<u>2</u>	<u>3.8</u>
	44	571.1
Service firms		
Management and investment (A. Soriano y Cia., Theo H. Davies, Boise Cascade*)	3	123.4
Insurance (Insurance Specialists,* E.E. Elser*)	2	.4
Media activities (Loreto F. de Henudes,* J. Walter Thompson,* McCann-Erickson*)	3	2.2
Other service enterprises (Airmac, Sanitary Steam Laundry, Phil. Edu., Inter-Island Constr., Pacific Airways,* Dean International*)	<u>6</u>	<u>11.5</u>
	14	137.5

	Number of firms	U.S. owned net worth (P million)
Public utilities		
Shipping and shipping agents (C.F. Sharp, Everett Steamship)	2	3.7
Telecommunications (ITT Phils.)	<u>1</u>	<u>1.2</u>
	3	4.9
Total, 165 largest, U.S., direct-investment, nonfinancial enterprises in the Philippines		P2,431.0
Financial enterprises		
Insurance (Phil.-Am. Life,* American Int. Underwriters*)	2	82.4[d]
Commercial banks (First National City Bank,* Bank of America*)	<u>2</u>	<u>153.1</u>
	4	235.5
Total, 169 largest, U.S., direct-investment enterprises in the Philippines		P2,666.5

Source: "Extent of American Investment in the Philippines in 1970," *Manila Chronicle*, 23 Nov. 1971. Also reprinted in the Philippine Economics Association's *Philippine Weekly Economic Review* 19 (30 Nov. 1971).

*Not included in "SEC-Business Day 1000 Top Philippine Corporations for 1970."

a.   U.S.-owned net worth of Caltex is divided equally between "manufacturing" and "commerce."

b.   The direct investment of Proctor and Gamble is confined to the wholly owned subsidiary, Philippine Manufacturing Company.

c.   Listed in the *Manila Chronicle* tabulation as Erlanger and Galinger.

d.   Assumes 100 percent U.S. ownership of Philippine-American Life.

Appendix B

United States Nonfinancial, Direct-
Investment Firms in Philippines
Ranked by U.S. Ownership Share of Net Worth, 1970
(P million, percent U.S.-owned net worth in parentheses)

Caltex (100)	330.6	
Benguet Consolidated (69)	208.5	
Mobil Oil (100)	170.2	
Atlas Consolidated (54)	141.0	
Bataan Refining (100)	101.5	951.8
A. Soriano y Compania (100)	90.5	
B.F. Goodrich (100)	76.9	
Philippine Packing (100)	73.1	
International Harvester-Macleod (100)	63.6	
Esso (100)	62.1	1,318.0
USIPHIL (100)	55.6	
Marcopper (41)	47.5	
Proctor and Gamble (100)	46.7	
Honiron Philippines (100)	40.0	
Bislig Bay Lumber (56)	35.7	
Firestone (75)	35.4	
Union Carbide (100)	35.3	
Goodyear (100)	34.9	
Theo H. Davies (90)	32.9	
Pepsi Cola Far East Trade Development (100)	31.2	1,713.2
Filoil Refining (67)	28.4	
General Milk (74)	24.2	
California Manufacturing (100)	22.9	
American Wire and Cable (100)	22.8	
Pepsi Cola Bottling (100)	22.2	
Hawaiian-Philippine (98)	19.5	
Colgate-Palmolive (100)	19.3	

Getty Oil (100)	18.1	
IBM Philippines (100)	17.2	
Coca Cola Export (100)	17.0	
Republic Glass (55)	15.0	
Phelps Dodge (61)	14.6	
Insular Lumber (97)	13.9	
Legaspi Oil (83)	13.5	
San Carlos Milling (66)	13.5	
Bogo Medellin Milling (92)	12.9	
Philippines Remnants (100)	12.7	
Gelmart Industries (99)	12.3	
Reynolds Philippines (51)	12.0	
Ault & Wiborg (100)	11.9	2,057.1

Source: "Extent of American Investment in the Philippines in 1970," *Manila Chronicle*, 23 Nov. 1971.   Also reprinted in the Philippine Economics Association's *Philippine Weekly Economic Review* 19 (30 Nov. 1971).

Notes

1. U.S. Philippine Commission, 1900-1916, *Report of the Philippine Commission . . . 1901*, 4 vols. (Washington, D.C.: Government Printing Office, 1901), 1:148-50.

2. U.S. Public Law (PL) 235, 1 July 1902, 32 Stat. 691.

3. For an informative account of the confusion and bureaucratic chicanery attending the transfer to American rule during 1898-1902, conditions which resulted in the establishment of legal claims to the lode and placer gold deposits worked by Filipinos from the ealiest of times, see Winifred L. Djajengwasito, "History of the Mining Industry in the Philippines, 1898-1941" (Ph.D. diss., Cornell University, 1972), 21-37.

4. U.S. PL 28, 8 Mar. 1902, 32 Stat. 11, sec. 5; U.S. PL 5, 5 Aug. 1909, 36 Stat. 11.

5. For the United States share of the average value of insular exports and imports, 1930-34, see Philippine Islands (P.I.), *Annual Report of the Collector of Customs, 1935* (Manila: Bureau of Printing, 1935).

6. U.S. Department of Commerce, Bureau of Foreign and Domestic Commerce, *American Direct Investments in Foreign Countries*, Trade Information Bulletin no. 731, November 1930.

7. Philippine Constitution, articles XII, XIII, and XIV; Philippines (Commonwealth), Commonwealth Act (CA) 137, 7 Nov. 1936; CA 141, 7 Nov. 1936. By the end of 1970, no fewer than twenty-eight Philippine laws established

173

Filipino nationality requirements for various economic activities; see *Study of Private Foreign Investments in the Philippines as of 12/31/1970* (Manila: Republic of the Philippines [R.P.], Inter-agency Working Group on Foreign Investments, 1971), annex A.

8. U.S. PL 370, 30 Apr. 1946, 60 Stat. 128; U.S. PL 371, 30 Apr. 1946, 60 Stat. 141.

9. Frank H. Golay, *The Philippines: Public Policy and National Economic Development* (Ithaca, N.Y.: Cornell University Press, 1961), 112.

10. Ibid., 128.

11. The U.S. Department of Commerce, *Survey of Current Business*, reports annually the value of American direct investment, defined as investment in enterprises with at least 25 percent American ownership.

12. R.P., Republic Act (RA) 1180, 19 June 1954; R.P., RA 3018, 2 Aug. 1960.

13. Frank H. Golay, Ralph Anspach, M. Ruth Pfanner, and Elizer B. Ayal, *Underdevelopment and Economic Nationalism in Southeast Asia* (Ithaca, N.Y.: Cornell University Press, 1971), 90-91.

14. Recent examples include the sale announced in May 1980 of 70 percent of the equity of Getty Philippines, Inc., the share remaining in American hands, to two Filipino firms. A year later, B.F. Goodrich announced the sale of its 54 percent stake in B.F. Goodrich Philippines, Inc., to a wholly owned subsidiary of Sime Darby of Malaysia. In mid-1983, Mobil Corporation, the third-largest foreign multinational in the Philippines, announced plans to "pull out" of the Philippines by selling its marketing facilities to Caltex Petroleum Corporation for $39.8 million and by transferring Mobil's 40 percent share in the Bataan Refining Corporation to the government-owned Philippine National

Oil Company at a price not specified. See *The
Philippine Newsletter* 1 (May 1980); *New York Times*,
10 June 1981, p. D5; and *Wall Street Journal*, 8 June
1983, p. 35.

15. Krivenko v. Register of Deeds of Manila, 79 Phil. 461
    (1947); Republic v. Quasha, 17 Aug. 1972, *Philippine
    Supreme Court Reports Annotated*, vol. 46.

16. R.P., RA 5816, 16 Sept. 1967.

17. U.S. Embassy, Manila, *Facts About RP-U.S. Relations* 2
    (10 Apr. 1970):2.

18. Shortly after taking office at the end of 1961,
    President Macapagal allowed the peso to float downward
    and in mid-1963 it was stabilized at P3.90 per U.S.
    dollar. This rate was maintained until early 1971 when
    President Marcos freed the peso to float a second time.
    Later in 1971 the American dollar was allowed to float
    and two years later the exchange rate of the peso was
    stabilized at P6.70 per U.S. dollar.

19. R.P., National Economic and Development Authority,
    Philippine Statistical Yearbook, 1978, 162-63, table
    4.10. If the calculated capital/output ratio had been
    more favorable for the Philippines--say 2.64, a very
    favorable ratio--the proportion of estimated Philippine
    capital stock at the end of 1977 represented by
    American direct investment would be 3.7 percent instead
    of 2.6 percent.

20. "SEC-*Business Day* 1000 Top Corporations in the
    Philippines, 1979," *Business Day* 11 (1979, special
    issue):14. The corporations listed are ranked by
    magnitude of sales.

21. Philippines (Commonwealth), Commission of the Census,
    Census of the Philippines: 1939--Real Property,
    Special Bulletin no. 3 (Manila: Bureau of Printing,

1941), 17, table 1; U.S. Embassy, Manila, *Facts About RP-US Relations* 4 (26 June 1970):1.

22. Lorenzo M. Tañada, *Nationalism: A Summons to Greatness* (Quezon City: Phoenix Publishing House, 1965), 61-62; R.P., NEDA, *Philippine Statistical Yearbook, 1978*, 243, 245, 249, tables 5.2 and 5.3. Commercial crops include coconuts, sugar cane, and native (cigar) tobacco.

23. *New York Times*, 29 May 1975.

24. *Policy Research* 1 (1 November 1974):4-5; R.P., Presidential Decree 471. For a comprehensive analysis of the resolution of issues raised by the Quasha decision, see Haru Landes and James E. Landes, "Divestment of U.S. Equity and Land Holdings in the Philippines, 1970-1976," part 3, *Aoyama Keizai Ronshu* [Aoyama economic review] 30 (April 1978):38-72 (in English).

PHILIPPINE-AMERICAN ECONOMIC INTERACTIONS:
A MATTER OF MAGNITUDE

Norman G. Owen

Ang banga ay di maaaring manalo sa tapayan

Tagalog proverb*

Historical writing on the economic relationships
between the Philippines and the United States has often
taken the form of a history of governmental policies and the
motives behind them.[1] From the start, most Americans
claimed the benevolence of their intentions, while anti-
imperialists and Filipino nationalists disputed that claim.
The records of public debates, to say nothing of the private
correspondence of officials, still make fascinating reading,
but it is by now clear that they do not suffice to explain
the uneven course of economic history. From the boom-or-
bust cycles of commodity prices to the persistent poverty of
the rural Philippines, what happened was often neither the
visible result of specific policies nor the intention of the
men who made those policies.

Recently a more structural approach has prevailed,
interpreting imperialism not simply as the taking of

---

*"A clay pot cannot win against a water jar." Damiana
L. Eugenio, *Philippine Proverb Lore* (Quezon City:
University of the Philippines, 1967), 378.

colonies, but as any subordinate relationship forced on a
weaker society by a stronger one. "Imperialism," thus
defined, does not start in 1898 or end in 1946 but pervades
and underlies the long-term relationship between an advanced
capitalist state and an agrarian society open to its
penetration. On the American side, such an approach helps
to explain, if any explanation is necessary, why actual
policy so often contradicted ostensible colonial aims.
Across the Pacific it helps to account for export
specialization, rising dependency on foreign markets,
political reinforcement of a collaborating Filipino elite
(or "comprador bourgeoisie"), and the failure of peasants to
benefit from putative prosperity.[2]

There is no doubt that such an approach can be
analytically useful in dealing with Philippine-American
economic interactions; it is equally clear that it leaves
unexplained certain discrepancies and paradoxes. If
American capitalism came to the Philippines with no other
end in mind than straightforward exploitation of Filipinos
for its own profit, then it did a poor job--at times
inefficient, at times absentminded, at times downright
contradictory, allowing Filipinos to profit at American
expense. On balance, of course, the net flow of resources
was from the Philippines to the United States, and it is
hard to dispute that American imperialism was responsible
for many of the economic problems the Philippines still
faces. Yet by comparison with such colonies as French
Indochina and the Netherlands Indies, the Philippines seems
to have escaped fairly lightly, suggesting that something
other than brute capitalism was at work.[3]

Efforts to explain these discrepancies generally take
one of two forms. Some emphasize the "special relationship"
and those qualities in American culture and politics--guilt,
altruism, legal scruples, etc.--which may have tempered
cruder economic drives. Others attempt to explain away each

apparent paradox as a materialist contradiction
misunderstood. Capitalism, they point out, is not
monolithic, and at times different capitalists will favor
differing strategies in the common struggle for profits.
Some seek markets for their manufactures, some seek outlet
for underemployed capital, some seek protection from
colonial imports, and all are capable of shifting tactics in
response to changes in the global economic environment.
Moreover, there are always some business and political
interests that insist on short-term profitability while
others, farther-sighted or better-heeled, are willing to
sacrifice immediate gains for long-term advantage.

Any comprehensive overview of Philippine-American
interactions must take into account both of these
perspectives; men do not act for economic motives alone, but
economic motives are also more complex than we sometimes
recognize. This essay, however, attempts no such overview.
Instead it identifies another factor in the equation, often
overlooked because it is so obvious: the factor of
magnitude. If we think only in terms of population, the
United States is today merely five times as large as the
Philippines, though it was ten times as large at the turn of
the century. But the trade of the United States is roughly
forty times as great as that of the Philippines and its
gross domestic product is more than eighty times as great.[4]
Disparities on this order are neither transient nor
incidental; they can influence the course of interactions as
surely as the disparity between a twenty-four-wheeled diesel
rig and a Volkswagen can influence the effects of a
collision between them.

*   *   *

By the mid-nineteenth century, long before Dewey sailed
into Manila Bay, the two unequal economies were already in
close contact. The commercial economy of the Bikol region
(in southeast Luzon), for example, was almost totally

dependent on the export of one crop--abaca, or Manila hemp--
to the markets of the United States and England. As those
markets rose and fell, they carried the Bikol economy with
them. As a result, the cycles of the American industrial
economy are visible in a variety of local indicators in the
region: land prices, wages, cockfight and town market
revenues, even marriage rates.[5] By the mid-1880s, shipments
of sugar to the United States accounted for nearly one-
quarter of the total value of exports from the Philippines,
yet the same shipments accounted for less than 1 percent of
the total value of United States imports. Despite some
fluctuations, throughout the late nineteenth century
Philippine-American trade was normally about thirty times as
valuable to the Philippines as it was to the United States.[6]

Formal American colonialism in the Philippines
increased the intensity of contact between the two economies
but hardly touched the basic disproportion. The ratio did
dip slightly in the 1930s, to about twenty-to-one; the
United States accounted for about 70 percent of all the
foreign trade of the Philippines, but this same commerce
amounted to some 3.5 percent of total American foreign
trade, a record high. By the 1950s, however, the ratio had
returned to thirty-to-one (60 percent of all Philippine
trade equaling 2 percent of American trade), and it remained
at the same level, though the percentages fell, in the
1970s. Whatever the commodity, whatever the price, whatever
the direction of the exchange, trade between the two
countries continues to be about thirty times more
significant to the Philippine economy than to the American.

The most obvious implication of this disproportion in
scale is a potential disproportion in power. The United
States has always had the capacity--intentionally or
inadvertently, benevolently or maliciously--to influence the
Philippine economy. The reverse is not generally true.
Philippine economic history can scarcely be written without

reference to American tariffs and fluctuations in the
American market for sugar, fibers, vegetable oils, and
minerals. Truer than the truism that "Whenever Washington
gets a cold, Manila sneezes" is the fact that whenever Wall
Street gets a cold, Makati sneezes. Even the current
export-oriented industrialization of the Philippines, as
Robert Snow notes, presumes continued access to the United
States; a new wave of protectionism here, whatever its
intentions, could virtually obliterate the growth in
electronics and textiles of which Marcos is so proud and on
which he counts so heavily.[7] Yet to the American economy,
both past and present, the Philippines is a mere footnote.

Such economic preponderance may, of course, be
translated directly into political leverage. Many scholars
have already studied the political history of the economic
relationship, though much still remains to be learned.
Controversy on both sides of the Pacific has surrounded key
events, from the Organic Act of 1902 through the Hare-Hawes-
Cutting Bill of 1932 to the surge of American aid after
martial law was declared in 1972. In a few instances the
United States flagrantly abused its economic preponderance,
particularly in the postwar period, when desperately needed
and repeatedly promised rehabilitation aid was withheld to
extort the "parity amendment" from the Philippines.[8] In
other instances the facts are as yet less clear or are
susceptible to conflicting interpretations; scholarly
analysis goes on.

Yet while scholars continue to debate over how wisely
or justly the United States used its power, the power itself
is the irreducible reality. Whatever the circumstances,
whatever the intentions of policymakers or the skills of
negotiators, the Philippines has remained "always in the
unenviable position of meaning infinitely less to the United
States than the United States meant to the Philippines."[9]
This imbalance of meaning, rooted in the imbalance of

magnitude, does not of course explain all the vagaries of
policy. But recognition of the inherent disproportion in
the Philippine-American relationship may help explain two
themes frequently noted in the literature: American
ambivalence and, to borrow Claro M. Recto's term, Filipino
mendicancy.[10]

The ambivalence, not to say ambiguity, of American
imperialism has been commented on by many scholars. The
unintended ironies of "benevolent assimilation" and the
"little brown brother" have been succeeded by more conscious
paradoxes: "imperialism of suasion," "cooperation and cross-
purposes," "permissive" colonialism, even "compadre
colonialism."[11] The recognition of this ambivalence does
not imply a denial that American imperialism had specific
characteristics, many of which were and are detrimental to
the Philippine economy. But it is clear to all but the most
fervent anticolonialist that the United States rarely if
ever had a real colonial "policy," in Webster's sense of the
word: "a settled course adopted or followed." The course of
American actions in the Philippines, though inspired in a
general sense by capitalism, was anything but "settled."
From the beginning, it was characterized by "neither wisdom
nor consistency," in the words of Richard Welch, Jr.[12]
Other historians of the early colonial period comment on the
"absence of concrete American plans," refer to "colonization
by improvisation," or claim flatly that "the United States
did not have an economic policy in the Philippines."[13]

Certain general principles may still be posited, of
course. The Philippines was encouraged (or forced) to
maintain a free market economy with which the United States
could trade and in which American capital could operate
freely. Toward this end the United States since 1898 has
felt free to intervene in Philippine politics, openly or
covertly, on behalf of pro-American leaders and probusiness
policies, throwing its considerable weight against any

perceived threat to the capitalist connection.[14] Yet no
sooner do we articulate these classic colonial and
neocolonial principles than we can think of exceptions.
Congress consistently thwarted most of the efforts of the
early Philippine Commission to facilitate American
investment in the colony. Later the colonial authorities
permitted in the Philippines a governmental role in the
economy that would have been rejected as "socialistic" had
it been proposed in the United States; they also allowed
foreign competitors, such as the Japanese, greater scope in
the Philippines than any other imperial power ever permitted
its commercial rivals. In the postwar period some Americans
urged retention, others separation; similarly there were
divisions on whether the Philippines should continue primary
production or attempt industrialization, peg the peso or
devaluate it, accept aid or seek self-sufficiency.[15]

Several lifetimes of scholarship may be necessary to
disentangle all the interests that conflicted and coalesced
to shape the hodge-podge of American actions in and toward
the Philippines. Yet underlying all the complex questions
is one simple fact: to the United States as a whole the
Philippines simply did not, and does not, matter. We do not
perceive our "vital national interests" at stake there. No
doubt there is an element of racism in this, as there has
been in almost all American dealings with Filipinos. But
decision-makers in the United States have ignored or
discounted not only the opinions of Filipinos but also those
of most Americans in the Philippines. The Philippine
Commission and the community of "Manila Americans" regularly
failed in their efforts to have their own retentionist
vision implemented by Congress, and they railed long and
hard against policies which (they claimed) injured Filipino
and American interests alike. Few of the governors general,
from Taft to Murphy, were ever entirely satisfied that the
United States was doing all it could or should for the
Philippine economy.[16] And in the postwar period, American

183

ambassadors, CIA agents, and businessmen have generally had more influence in Malacañan than in the White House. There is no significant instance of the United States shaping its basic economic policies to fit the realities of the Philippines, even as these were perceived and defined by local Americans.

The fundamental disproportion of scale is a major reason that the Philippines has always, from the beginning, been peripheral to the United States. Even the vocal imperialists and anti-imperialists during the Philippine-American War failed to sustain their debate with any intensity; the issue eventually was abandoned, rather than resolved.[17] To the extent that Americans in the Philippines were identified with the periphery of America's formal or informal empire, they tended to lose influence in the core, where real decisions were made. No professional civil service was created, and the Bureau of Insular Affairs, though characterized by one historian as "America's Colonial Desk," was but a pale shadow of the Colonial Office in London.[18]

Thus America's colonial and postcolonial policy acquired its ambivalence. It was never the product of a conscious and continuous decision-making process, much less of national will or purpose. Instead it was created by a shifting series of ad hoc coalitions of interests that happened--at a particular time, on a particular issue--to care about a situation that did not greatly concern the United States as a whole. This of course offered opportunities for the exercise of very considerable leverage. Even a small force, exerted at the right point, might swing the whole massive weight of America toward or away from the Philippines. Not surprisingly, given the structure of corporate America, such forces often represented business interests. But most American businessmen were also relatively indifferent to the

Philippines, so at times one firm, perhaps even one man
(Elihu Root and Paul McNutt come to mind) might be in a
position to shape or alter American policy--which accounts
for some of its inconsistency. Whether or not a more
consistent policy would have benefited the Filipinos or
merely exploited them more systematically is a matter for
speculation.

If American ambivalence may be attributed in part to
the fact that the Philippines mattered very little, Filipino
mendicancy may be attributed in part to the fact that the
United States mattered too much. Even the Nacionalista
heroes of the colonial period came to power with the aid of
American patrons and repeatedly shied away from rapid and
real independence, opting instead to retain a political
connection that meant, among other things, preferred access
for Philippine goods in the American market.[19] Political
independence has scarcely altered this relationship, as one
government after another, despite nationalist rhetoric, has
shown its reluctance to break with the United States. "A
bankrupt administration must necessarily have a foreign
policy of mendicancy," said Recto in 1951, ". . . and
because beggars cannot be choosers, we can be safely
ignored, taken for granted, dictated to, and made to wait at
the door, hat in hand, to go in only when invited."[20]
Though time has altered a few details, the same accusations
continue to be made more than a quarter of a century
later.[21] Filipino patriots may--and should--debate the
political ethics of the decisions and indecisions of their
elected leaders. Historians may appropriately attempt to
analyze the phenomenon of mendicancy in its context, which
includes the factor of magnitude.

The Filipino political elite, nearly always intelligent
(whatever else may be said of them), have from the beginning
perceived not only the might of American arms and the
seductiveness of American culture, but also the importance

of the United States to the Philippine capitalist economy
and thus also to their own individual and class interests.
Imperialism forcibly brought the two countries together and
allowed the larger economy to penetrate and dominate the
smaller. It was the role of the elite, as they perceived it
themselves, to make the best of the situation; this implied
accepting, and attempting to manipulate, the dependency
inherent in the disproportion of scale.

Once this dependent relationship was accepted, it was
logically consistent for Filipinos, from the Federalistas of
the 1900s to the technocrats of the 1980s, to take advantage
of whatever opportunities existed within the unequal
partnership. The Federalistas' advocacy of annexation, the
rise of the sugar bloc (with its perpetual and generally
successful lobbying for larger quotas in the United States),
and the extensive borrowing in the postwar period, even when
the loans have had visible strings, all might be interpreted
this way. So might the paradox of Marcos actively
soliciting American investment in the hope--he says--that he
can build thereby an industrial base which may in time
enable the Philippines to be economically independent at
last.

The alternatives, for many Filipino leaders, have been
almost literally inconceivable. Unlike the revolution
against Spain, which was physically dangerous but involved
little social or economic readjustment,[22] a revolution
against the United States, at first militarily unwinnable,
soon became economically unthinkable. Too many Filipinos
produced goods that could be sold with profit only in the
United States; too many of the imports and investments
Filipinos had come to require were of American origin. Real
independence would have jeopardized all this as well as
risking possible direct reprisals, while any "independence"
that left intact the power of American capital to penetrate

the Philippines would also leave intact a relationship of dependency of the weaker economy on the stronger.

In this respect, at least, the "Americanists" in the Philippines were often more realistic or honest than their nominally nationalist rivals. The latter persisted in claiming that the Philippines could enjoy independence without paying any significant price. Yet the price was and is real. The cessation of trade with and aid from the United States would be a tremendous shock to capitalism as it now exists in the Philippines, a shock from which it might not recover. A "sequestered" free-enterprise economy is theoretically possible, but is unlikely to prosper in the short run, as the technocrats well know. True independence for the Philippines, then, would involve *radical* change, and there is a sense in which the "Americanists" have been honest in recognizing and opposing this.

There have, of course, also been some Filipinos who would have accepted or even welcomed the radical reorientation of the economy real independence implied. Some looked backward to idyllic communalism, some looked forward to a version of socialism, some were simply willing to pay any cost to be free of foreign domination. But from Macario Sakay and Felipe Salvador through the Huks and the student movement to the National Democratic Front, their voices have been suppressed, in part by Americans, in part by Filipinos who feared that they might offend the Americans.[23] The dominant propensity in twentieth-century Philippine politics has been to respond to the United States as a poor peasant might to a powerful landlord—at times grateful, at times resentful, but always acutely aware of the great disproportion that lies between them.

Certainly the factor of magnitude does not by itself account for the contrast between Filipino and American attitudes towards their mutual interaction. By comparison with Americans, Filipinos believe in the "special relationship" more deeply, worry about it more persistently, and curse more roundly when it is betrayed.[24] This imbalance of concern is not easy to interpret; few confidential records have survived, and in the very nature of unequal relationships it is often in the interest of the weaker party to conceal true feelings even from supposed friends. We must, of course, take into account the direct role of the United States in shaping Filipino values through education ("miseducation," in Renato Constantino's view) and through reinforcement of pro-American leaders and repression of anti-American alternatives.[25] Cultural variables also may be included; like other Southeast Asians, Filipinos are inclined to personalize economics (as in the *suki* relationship), while Westerners tend to cleave to the adage that "business is business."[26] Yet even where neither colonialism nor culture can explain it, an inverse intensity of concern may accompany an enormous disproportion of scale; witness the obsession of many Canadians with the United States in contrast with our vast indifference to our northern neighbor.

*   *   *

Though the political history of Philippine-American economics may be difficult to analyze, at least its outlines are known. On the other hand, the history of business-- through which the disproportion of scale was actually mediated--is virtually *terra incognita*. Not only are business records less accessible to historians, but the subject has generally been less intriguing to them as well. Businesses, we assume, seek assiduously to maximize profits by all legal means and may even bend or break the law whenever they think they can get away with it. Thus there is little of the dramatic discrepancy between professed ideals and actual policy that so enlivens the history of governments. (Businessmen do profess ethics, of course, but no one takes this too seriously.) Without this inherent drama, business history can easily become no more than a register of company officials and a chronicle of profits and losses, scarcely of interest to anyone outside the firm studied.

The few and valiant efforts to write the history of Philippine-American business interactions have tended to be--as pioneering research often is--either so general as to be superficial or so firm-specific that no larger context is visible. More and deeper studies are certainly needed, and there are signs that some may be forthcoming.[27] In the interim, discussing the significance of magnitude in Philippine-American business history is less a matter of interpreting existing scholarship than of suggesting what future scholars might look for.

During the nineteenth century two Americans firms-- Russell & Sturgis and Peele, Hubbell & Co.--made significant contributions to the development of a Philippine export economy. They created, in the words of Benito Legarda, Jr., "the nexus between the Philippine economy and the currents of world trade."[28] By regular cultivation of foreign markets (especially the United States and England) they helped stimulate the demand for Philippine produce; by skillful mobilization of local capital they helped stimulate the production to meet that demand. At times the two firms handled more than half the insular output of the two most important export crops, sugar and abaca. One twenty-five-year-old American clerk in Albay, in fact, purchased for their "joint account" one-third of the entire abaca production of the Philippines in 1862-63.[29]

The partners of Peele, Hubbell & Co. conformed in general to the business ethic of their day. They worked hard, they were honest according to their lights, and they tried to be fair with each other and with their agents and brokers. They also, however, tried very hard to create an oligopsony in abaca, with the intention of driving down the

local price to just what it would pay cultivators to
continue growing it; the result, as one of them put it,
would be to make "more Money . . . for white people."[30] If
exploitation is defined as taking from the worker most of
the real value of what he produces, leaving him barely
enough to live on, then Peele, Hubbell & Co. clearly aspired
to be exploiters. In fairness, although they regularly
maligned the Filipinos and attempted to exploit them, they
also denigrated the Spaniards and a fair number of English
and American merchants, making every effort to profit at
their expense as well. Like most men of their time, they
were racist, but racism was not the issue. Capitalism was.

Yet the final winners in this encounter were not the
American merchants. Russell & Sturgis went bankrupt in
1875; Peele, Hubbell & Co. followed in 1887. Nor were the
final losers the abaca cultivators of Albay, whose standard
of living actually seems to have risen slightly during the
nineteenth century. This is not to deny that substantial
profits were remitted to the United States or even that the
cordage-makers and farmers of the United States enjoyed
cheaper fiber than they might otherwise have obtained. The
opportunity costs to the Filipinos should not be ignored,
though they are all but impossible to calculate. Who can
tell what profits, if any, there would have been without the
Americans or how these might or might not have been invested
in local development? Nevertheless, the exploitation of
Filipinos by nineteenth-century American merchants was
relatively inefficient as such matters go.

Part of the difficulty faced by these firms was a
matter of magnitude. Each was nominally capitalized at less
than a million dollars and was considerably overextended
much of the time. Each had borrowed heavily and was able to
repay old loans only through almost constant success in new
ventures. Neither could dominate the abaca trade directly;
even when they pooled their endeavors in the "joint account"

they could not run off their British and Spanish rivals nor get them to join the cartel. Neither had great political influence within the Philippines; they may have befriended a few provincial officials and even bribed a few judges, but they could not shape colonial policy. Finally, neither had any significant economic interests outside the Philippines. Their fortunes, like those of other local firms, rose and fell with the Philippine economy as a whole. In their immediate profit-seeking they always had to be careful not to destroy the industries on which their profits ultimately depended.[31]

Although these two firms eventually collapsed, the tradition of local American business which they had pioneered did not vanish forever. After 1898 new firms were created--Lusteveco and Benguet Consolidated among the most prominent--which became equally significant in the economic history of the Philippines.[32] More research on how American businessmen differed from their Filipino and Chinese rivals might be useful; the values and business practices of the Philippines today, like its cuisine, represent an amalgam of local and alien traditions. Yet in one important respect these firms resembled their twentieth-century rivals as well as their nineteenth-century predecessors. Both their financial leverage and their political clout were limited by their size and by their location on the periphery of the American empire. They may have appeared to be pretty big fish, but they were no larger than the pond in which they were bred.

At the same time, however, some truly big fish began to enter Philippine waters--the "multinational" American corporations. In scale and scope these were quite unlike anything the Philippines had known before.[33] In 1904, Macleod & Company, a British merchant house, was bought for $190,000 by International Harvester Company, a corporation capitalized at some $120 million--over six-hundred times the

size of its new acquisition--and backed by credit from both
J. P. Morgan and John D. Rockefeller. Within seven years
Macleod had more than doubled in value and was handling over
one-third of all the abaca exports of the Philippines. But
the $5.5 million worth of abaca Macleod exported, which
accounted for about one-eighth of the total exports of the
Philippines, amounted to just one-tenth of the total
business of the parent firm. By this criterion
International Harvester mattered more to the Philippines
than the Philippines mattered to International Harvester.[34]

International Harvester may have employed its size to
the disadvantage of the Philippines in two different ways,
if its critics can be believed. First, the firm was a
leader in the lobby of American fiber importers and cordage
makers that successfully urged the establishment and
subsequently fought the repeal of an export tax on
Philippine abaca and a rebate of that tax to whoever
imported abaca into the United States. In effect this
amounted to a Philippine subsidy of the American cordage
industry, yet the protests of both colonial officials and
Filipino politicians were regularly ignored by the
U.S. Congress, which was more disposed to listen to the
domestic lobby. According to one calculation, over
$4 million was diverted from Filipino producers or the
insular treasury to the pockets of American importers
between 1902 and 1910.[35]

Second, International Harvester, according to some
colonial officials, deliberately induced the great
depression in abaca prices that began in 1907 and lasted
until World War I. The truth of this allegation, more
serious than the former, has not to my knowledge been
established. It is now known that in 1902 International
Harvester entered into a secret agreement with the governor
of Yucatan (Mexico) to depress artificially the price of
sisal hemp, the chief determinant of world hard fiber

prices.[36] But it is also clear that another cause for the decline in abaca in 1907 was a major industrial slump in the United States, for which International Harvester can scarcely be blamed.

Though further research is clearly called for, it may be impossible to ascertain the truth of these allegations or assess with any precision the damage International Harvester may have done. It is significant, however, that the allegations are plausible. Unlike local firms, the center of gravity of International Harvester lay elsewhere; its corporate interests might well have been served by sabotaging the Philippine abaca industry. And it had-- again, unlike local firms--the potential leverage to do so, to buy influence in Washington and Mexico, to influence markets by collusion or even by sheer weight. Any deeper historical investigation of the role played by International Harvester in the economic history of the Philippines will have to take into account the factor of magnitude.

The same general considerations might apply to other giant American corporate interests in the Philippines, from the Hawaiian sugar bloc to the First National City Bank. They had both global interests which might at times override their Philippine concerns and the scale to take effective action on behalf of these interests. Standard Vacuum Oil Company, for example, was founded in 1933 as the joint Far Eastern subsidiary of Socony Vacuum (the forerunner of Mobil) and Standard Oil of New Jersey (the forerunner of Exxon). The nearly two million barrels of petroleum products Stanvac sold in the Philippines in 1939 accounted for about 45 percent of local consumption, yet represented just two-thirds of one percent of the total global production of the parent companies. Stanvac had some $6.7 million invested in the Philippines at the outbreak of World War II. This represented 2.2 percent of its investments in East and Southeast Asia, 1.5 percent of the

total foreign investments in the Philippines, but just
0.2 percent of the combined assets of Socony and Standard of
New Jersey, which approached $3 billion--nearly nine times
the total commodity output of the Philippines![37]

By 1980, the Ford Motor Company had $45 million
invested in the Philippines, an important component in local
industrialization plans. Yet this $45 million also amounted
to just 0.2 percent of the company's global assets, and
compared unfavorably with the $2.5 billion a year Ford was
investing in capital expenditures in North America, the
$1.2 billion Ford spent in Spain before a single car was
produced, or even the $700 million Ford *lost* on the Edsel.
Ford, whose total assets of $23.5 billion approximate in
magnitude the entire gross domestic product of the
Philippines, supplies about one-third of all motor vehicles
sold throughout the entire region of Southeast Asia, yet
this fleet of Fieras represents less than one-third of one
percent of Ford's global production of vehicles.[38]

The sheer size of such firms as these does not, of
course, indicate that they abused their power or exploited
the Filipinos. But it does raise questions. In the
aftermath of World War II, the three major prewar oil
importers were reimbursed for a large portion of their war
losses (by the American taxpayers) and given the exclusive
right to distribute all petroleum products in the
Philippines for a fee of ten cents a liter above cost (at
the expense of Filipino consumers). Was this compensation--
more substantial than that received by most war-ravaged
Filipinos--in any way a function of their magnitude?[39]
Thirty years later it was alleged that Henry Ford II
accepted a $2 million bribe to build a Fiera stamping plant
in the Philippines. Is this simply another proof that the
rulers of the Philippines need the Ford Motor Company more
than Ford needs the Philippines? Or does scale, in this
case, work the other way, tending to exonerate Ford? Why

would the man or the company risk accepting a bribe in conjunction with anything as petty, from their perspective, as the Philippines?[40]

Focusing on possible abuses of power, however, may distract our attention from the problems that large firms potentially pose to the Philippine economy even when they are neither breaking nor bending the law. They simply matter too much. If Intel or Levi Strauss should decide-- for perfectly honorable reasons--to disinvest from the Philippines (or refuse to market the products of its subsidiaries and subcontractors, which would be much the same), a sizable pocket of unemployment and a sharp drop in export earnings would be expected. Should the Ford Motor Company or the First National City Bank express unhappiness with a tax proposal, could the government of the Philippines really afford to offend them and risk losing their investments? It might be assumed that fruit companies (Dole, Del Monte, United Fruit), with their greater investments in land and physical capital, would have less propensity to flee, but they came to the Philippines after abandoning other locations where business and labor conditions were insufficiently favorable, and presumably they could take flight again.

The argument is not simply that small is beautiful or even less ugly than big. Obviously there may be substantial differences among businesses of all sizes in stability, employment patterns, and short-run and long-run contributions to national development (export potential, diversification, etc.), to say nothing of ethics. Yet to ignore scale and focus exclusively on comparative business practices would be as foolish as analyzing the comparative skills of two boxers while failing to point out that one is a featherweight, the other a super-heavyweight. We may rejoice at the tale of David and Goliath, but the wisdom of

Las Vegas remains: Bet on Goliath! For better or worse, size matters.

*   *   *

Finally, recognition of the factor of magnitude may alter our perspective on imperialism in its many varieties. Certainly a small nation may impose its will on a larger one. "God gave the Portuguese," as the proverb has it, "only a small country to be born in, but the whole world in which to die." In the modern era the disproportion of scale between the Netherlands and the Indies or between Belgium and the Congo has been predominantly in favor of the colony. Yet these tend to be precisely the colonial relationships most characterized by formality, rigidity, niggardliness, and tightly controlled imperial preference, as the metropolitan powers found they could only obtain profits by systematic regulation.

The greater the disproportion in favor of the colonial power, however, the more likely the relationship will resemble the "imperialism of free trade," which has been the predominant theme in Philippine-American interactions since the nineteenth century. Governments have come and gone, but under Spanish rule, American rule, and Filipino rule American business has enjoyed essentially unrestricted access to the Philippine economy. The results are largely explicable in terms of disproportion; the United States has not needed a whole panoply of arbitrary restrictions to dominate the Philippine economy. At times, as we have seen, American interests have indeed sought additional advantages--a tariff here, a rebate there--and at times local interests have fought back by restricting some of the activities of American business.[41] But these are merely variations on the central theme--once the door was opened for capitalism, magnitude did the rest.

The other great constant of Philippine economic history over the past century is the persistent poverty of the great

majority of Filipinos. Historians may debate over whether
and when levels of living rose or fell slightly (with peaks
in the 1910s and 1960s?), but it would be hard to prove that
the material welfare of the average Filipino is
significantly higher today than it was in the nineteenth
century. Recent studies indicate that the level of
nutrition in the Philippines is among the worst in Asia,
second only to Bangladesh; international agencies estimate
that 50 to 80 percent of all Filipino children are seriously
malnourished.[42] Any study of the Philippine economy which
fails to take this into account is disingenuous at best.

It is possible, of course, that this poverty is simply
coincidental, explicable in terms of inadequate resources,
short-sighted leadership, or just plain bad luck. Yet seen
over the span of a century in which the poverty and the
Philippine-American relationship are constants, it is
difficult not to assume that they are somehow connected.
Whatever its motives, whatever the specific policies it
included, the "special relationship" has not proved healthy
for the Filipinos. The juxtaposition of the two capitalist
economies, imposed by imperialism, allowed the larger and
stronger to dominate the smaller and weaker. This was true
even when no evil was intended. Once imperialism had
established the connection, the Philippines came to depend
on an American domestic economy that was scarcely conscious
of the existence of these distant islands, much less of its
effect on them. To read the reports of colonial officials
or postcolonial economic advisors during any of the numerous
twentieth-century depressions or recessions is to realize
their helplessness in the face of such structural problems.
When the American fiber market plummeted, no official,
colonial or indigenous, could save the Philippine abaca
industry or those who depended upon it.

Ultimately, of course, the relationship has always been
asymmetrical, despite occasional efforts to create a nominal

reciprocity. Perhaps this must always be the case; when two
"partners" are so unequal, is real partnership possible?[43]
It may be that the greatest good the United States could
have done for the Philippines would have been to leave it
alone. Possibly the wisest policy for the Philippines would
have been some form of sequestration (if the United States
had permitted it), regardless of the short-term costs.
Focusing on the disproportion of magnitude does not prove
that the relationship was inherently unhealthy, but it
creates a strong, and sad, presumption.

Notes

1. See, for example, José S. Reyes, *Legislative History of
    America's Economic Policy Toward the Philippines* (New
    York: Columbia University, 1923); Jose P. Apostol, "The
    American-Philippine Tariff," *Philippine Social Science
    Review*, 1930-32 passim; Pedro E. Abelarde, *American
    Tariff Policy Towards the Philippines: 1898-1946* (New
    York: King's Crown Press, 1947); Shirley Jenkins,
    American Economic Policy Toward the Philippines
    (Stanford: Stanford University Press, 1954); cf.
    A. V. H. Hartendorp, *History of Industry and Trade in
    the Philippines* (Manila: American Chamber of Commerce,
    1958), which, despite its title, is more a history of
    economic policy than of economics.

2. For a variety of Marxist and non-Marxist versions of
    this approach, see William J. Pomeroy, *American Neo-
    Colonialism: Its Emergence in the Philippines and Asia*
    (New York: International Publishers, 1970); Jose
    Ma. Sison [Amado Guerrero], *Philippine Society and
    Revolution* (Manila: Pulang Tala Publications, 1971);
    Alejandro Lichauco, *The Lichauco Paper: Imperialism in
    the Philippines* (New York: Monthly Review Press, 1973);
    Walden Bello and Severino Rivera, eds., *The Logistics
    of Repression and Other Essays* (Washington, D.C.:

Friends of the Filipino People, 1977); Jonathan Fast
and Jim Richardson, *Roots of Dependency: Political and
Economic Revolution in 19th Century Philipines* (Quezon
City: Foundation for Nationalist Studies, 1979); and
Stephen Rosskamm Shalom, *The United States and the
Philippines: A Study of Neocolonialism* (Philadelphia:
Institute for the Study of Human Issues, 1981). A
useful introduction to general theory and debate in
this area is Aidan Foster-Carter, "From Rostow to
Gunder Frank: Conflicting Paradigms in the Analysis of
Underdevelopment," *World Development* 4 (March 1976):
167-80; see also Charles W. Bergquist, *Alternative
Approaches to the Problem of Development: A Selected
and Annotated Bibliography* (Durham, N.C.: Carolina
Academic Press, 1979).

3. Frank H. Golay, "Southeast Asia: The 'Colonial Drain'
    Revisited," in *Southeast Asian History and
    Historiography*, ed. C. D. Cowan and O. W. Wolters
    (Ithaca: Cornell University Press, 1976), 368-87,
    provides some comparative data.

4. United Nations, *Statistical Yearbook: 1978* (New York:
    United Nations, 1979).

5. Norman G. Owen, *Prosperity Without Progress: Manila
    Hemp and Material Life in the Colonial Philippines*
    (Berkeley: University of California Press,
    forthcoming).

6. Benito Fernandez Legarda, Jr., "Foreign Trade, Economic
    Change, and Entrepreneurship in the Nineteenth Century
    Philippines" (Ph.D. diss., Harvard University, 1955).

7. Robert T. Snow, "Export-oriented Industrialization, the
    International Division of Labor, and the Rise of the
    Subcontract Bourgeoisie in the Philippines," in this
    volume.

8. Hernando J. Abaya, *Betrayal in the Philippines* (1946; reprint, Quezon City: Malaya Books, 1970), 175-205; Jenkins, *American Economic Policy*, 42-96; Shalom, *United States and the Philippines: Neocolonialism*, 33-67; Frank H. Golay, "Economic Consequences of the Philippine Trade Act," *Pacific Affairs* 28 (Mar. 1955):53-70.

9. Claude A. Buss, "Introduction," in Jenkins, *American Economic Policy*, 21.

10. Claro M. Recto, "Our Mendicant Foreign Policy," in Teodoro A. Agoncillo, *Filipino Nationalism, 1872-1970* (Quezon City: R. P. Garcia Publishing Co., 1974), 321-46 (article first published in 1951). See David Wurfel, "Problems of Decolonization," in *The United States and the Philippines*, ed. Frank H. Golay (Englewood Cliffs, N.J.: Prentice-Hall, 1966), 154-55, on the connection between inequality of size/status and Filipino "emotionalism" in dealing with the United States.

11. Peter W. Stanley, *A Nation in the Making: The Philippines and the United States, 1899-1921* (Cambridge: Harvard University Press, 1974), 265-78; Mamerto S. Ventura, *United States-Philippine Cooperation and Cross-Purposes: Philippine Post-War Recovery and Reform* (Quezon City: Filipiniana Publications, 1974); Grant K. Goodman, "America's 'Permissive' Colonialism: Japanese Business in the Philippines, 1899-1941," in this volume; Norman G. Owen, ed., *Compadre Colonialism: Studies on the Philippines Under American Rule*, Michigan Papers on South and Southeast Asia, no. 3 (Ann Arbor: Center for South And Southeast Asian Studies, The University of Michigan, 1971).

12. *Webster's New Collegiate Dictionary*, s.v. "policy"; Richard E. Welch, Jr., *Response to Imperialism: The*

United States and the Philippine-American War,
1899-1902 (Chapel Hill: University of North Carolina
Press, 1979), 155.

13. Bonifacio S. Salamanca, *The Filipino Response to*
American Rule, 1901-1913 (Hamden, Conn.: Shoestring
Press, 1968), 185; Salvador P. Lopez, "The Colonial
Relationship," in Golay, *United States and the*
Philippines, 8; Glenn Anthony May, *Social Engineering*
in the Philippines: The Aims, Execution, and Impact of
American Colonial Policy, 1900-1913 (Westport, Conn.:
Greenwood Press, 1980), 129. See also Theodore Friend,
Between Two Empires: The Ordeal of the Philippines,
1929-1946 (New Haven: Yale University Press, 1965), 5
("American economic policies worked at cross purposes:
some prompted self-reliance and others fostered
dependence"); Sidney Fine, *Frank Murphy: The New Deal*
Years (Chicago: University of Chicago Press, 1979), 5
("American policy in the Philippines tended to
emphasize first one and then the other of the twin
objectives of American rule"). Though Shalom attempts
to argue that American neocolonialism in the
Philippines was conscious and programmatic, he also
provides evidence that on certain questions American
"policymakers were seriously divided" (p. 38).

14. Shalom is the most articulate exponent of this
argument, especially for the period 1944-54, but the
point is also made by most other serious scholars of
the relationship, and the fact of American involvement
in the politics of the "independent" Philippines is
acknowledged by all. On Philippine politics under
American colonialism, see the sources cited in notes 19
and 23 below.

15. May, *Social Engineering*, 129-75; Golay, "'Manila
Americans' and Philippine Policy: The Voice of American
Business," in this volume; Stanley, *Nation in the*

Making, 226-48; Friend, *Between Two Empires*, 151, 159;
Leo C. Stine, "The Economic Policies of the
Commonwealth Government of the Philippine Islands,"
University of Manila Journal of East Asiatic Studies 10
(March 1966):1-136; Goodman, "'Permissive'
Colonialism"; Hartendorp, *History of Industry*, 49-60;
Jenkins, *American Economic Policy*; Shalom, *United
States and the Philippines: Neocolonialism*.

16. U.S. War Department, Bureau of Insular Affairs, *Report
of the Philippine Commission*, 1900-1916 passim; Golay,
"'Manila Americans' and Philippine Policy"; May, *Social
Engineering*, 142-43, 153-60, 174; Fine, *Frank Murphy*,
119-54.

17. Welch, *Response to Imperialism*, supersedes or refutes
most of Daniel B. Schirmer, *Republic or Empire*
(Cambridge, Mass.: Schenkman Publishing Co., 1972) and
provides a fascinating compendium of the views of
American politicians, businessmen, labor leaders,
churchmen, and intellectuals, showing in case after
case how interest in the Philippines flagged a year or
two after annexation. It was not an issue which
produced sustained commitment--for or against
imperialism--in any but a tiny minority; the majority
soon acceded to the fact of American colonialism, for
better or worse.

18. Romeo V. Cruz, *America's Colonial Desk and the
Philippines, 1898-1934* (Quezon City: University of the
Philippines, 1974). It is interesting to note that
except for Taft no American governor general or high
commissioner (much less any chief of the Bureau of
Insular Affairs or ambassador to the Philippines)
succeeded in using the post as a springboard to the
presidency, though several entertained such ambitions.
Apparently most Americans were not impressed with the
colonial experience the Philippines provided.

19. Michael Cullinane, "The Politics of Collaboration in
     Tayabas Province: The Early Political Career of Manuel
     Quezon, 1903-1906," and "'Osmeña Is King and All Is
     Well': Philippine-American Politics, 1898-1907," both
     forthcoming; Friend, *Between Two Empires*, 34-148;
     Theodore Friend, "Manuel Quezon: Charismatic
     Conservative," *Philippine Historical Review* 1, no. 1
     (1965):153-69; Joseph F. Hutchinson, Jr., "Quezon's
     Role in Philippine Independence," in Owen, *Compadre
     Colonialism*, 157-94; Renato Constantino, *The
     Philippines: A Past Revisited* (Manila: Tala Publishing
     Co., 1975), 308-41.

20. Recto, "Mendicant," 335-36.

21. Renato Constantino and Letizia R. Constantino, *The
     Philippines: The Continuing Past* (Quezon City:
     Foundation for Nationalist Studies, 1978), 269-344;
     William J. Pomeroy, *An American-Made Tragedy: Neo-
     Colonialism & Dictatorship in the Philippines* (New
     York: International Publishers, 1974), 17-67, 91-128;
     Renato Constantino, "Real Independence Is Still Not Yet
     Complete," *Far Eastern Economic Review*, 17 Nov. 1978;
     "U.S.-R.P. Relations Under the Carter Administration--
     An Analysis," *Philippine Liberation Courier*, 25 Mar.
     1979; Shalom, *United States and the Philippines:
     Neocolonialism*, 86-144, 161-82. Critics charge that
     the shift in borrowing from the United States to the
     American-dominated World Bank and International
     Monetary Fund alters only the form, and not the
     structure, of Philippine dependency; Walden Bello,
     "Development and Dictatorship: Marcos and the World
     Bank," in Bello and Rivera, *Logistics of Repression*,
     93-133; Cheryl Payer, *The Debt Trap: the IMF and the
     Third World* (Harmondsworth, Middlesex: Penguin Books,
     1974), 50-74.

22. Milagros Camayon Guerrero, "Luzon at War: Contradictions in Philippine Society, 1898-1902" (Ph.D. diss., University of Michigan, 1977), shows how radical tendencies within the Philippine revolution were systematically undercut and eventually extirpated by Aguinaldo and the *ilustrados*.

23. On Sakay and Salvador, see Reynaldo Clemeña Ileto, *Pasyon and Revolution: Popular Movements in the Philippines, 1840-1910* (Quezon City: Ateneo de Manila University Press, 1979), 197-313; on other radical elements in the Philippine Revolution, see Guerrero, "Luzon at War." The decision of the Filipino elite to repress radicalism for fear that it might jeopardize relations with the United States can be seen most clearly in the decision to refuse to seat the Democratic Alliance Congressmen elected in 1946, which enabled Manuel Roxas to ram the "parity amendment" through Congress and thus preserve rehabilitation aid from the United States; Ronald King Edgerton, "The Politics of Reconstruction in the Philippines: 1945-1948" (Ph.D. diss., University of Michigan, 1975), 356-67 and passim; Shalom, *United States and the Philippines: Neocolonialism*, 51-59.

24. Wurfel, "Problems of Decolonization," 149-55.

25. Renato Constantino, "The Miseducation of the Filipino," in Renato Constantino, *The Filipinos in the Philippines and Other Essays* (1966; reprint, Quezon City: Malaya Books, 1971), 39-65; see also "Our Captive Minds," in ibid., 66-80. Perhaps the most notorious examples of Americans who simultaneously supported their Filipino friends and suppressed their Filipino enemies are Colonel Harry Hill Bandholtz of the Philippine Constabulary, patron of Quezon and pursuer of Sakay, and Colonel Edwin Geary Lansdale of the CIA, patron of Magsaysay and pursuer of the Huks.

26. Maria Cristina Blanc Szanton, *A Right to Survive: Subsistence Marketing in a Lowland Philippine Town* (University Park: Pennsylvania State University Press, 1972); Ogden Ellery Edwards (of Peele, Hubbell & Co.) to George Henry Peirce (of the same), 8 May 1864, Peirce Family Papers, Stanford University Libraries.

27. Two examples of such pioneering works, both valuable within their limits, are Lewis E. Gleeck, Jr., *American Business and Philippine Economic Development* (Manila: Carmelo & Bauermann, 1975), and Maria Teresa Colayco, *The Ropemakers: The Story of Manila Cordage Company* (Manila: n.p., 1975). A potential upswing in business history is suggested not only by the series of colloquia at the University of Michigan at which the papers in this volume were originally given, but also by a panel on "Philippine Business History" at the First International Philippine Studies Conference, Kalamazoo, 29 May – 1 June 1980.

28. Legarda, "Foreign Trade," 361-62.

29. Benito Fernandez Legarda, "American Entrepreneurs in the 19th Century Philippines" *Bulletin of the American Historical Collection* [Manila] 1, no. 1 (June 1972), 25-52 (article first published in 1957); Norman G. Owen, "Americans in the Abaca Trade: Peele, Hubbell & Co., 1856-1875," forthcoming.

30. Richard Dalton Tucker to Peirce, 21 Apr. 1868, Peirce Family Papers.

31. Owen, "Americans in the Abaca Trade."

32. Gleeck, *American Business*, provides an introduction to these and other firms; see also Morton J. Netzorg, "A View From the Pasig," *Bulletin of the American Historical Collection* 9 (Jan.-Mar. 1981):6-30, on his experiences with Lusteveco in the 1920s, and Edilberto C. de Jesús, "John Haussermann and Benguet

Mining Company," an unpublished paper from the 1980 Kalamazoo conference. The *American Chamber of Commerce Journal*, now the *AmCham Journal*, has been the voice of the American merchant community in Manila for over half a century.

33. Actually, the first such "multinationals" in the Philippines were probably the Chartered Bank of India, Australia & China and the Hongkong & Shanghai Bank, which opened branches in Manila in 1872 and 1875, respectively, but both seem to have confined themselves to banking and did not engage directly in either industry or trade. See Compton Mackenzie, *Realms of Silver: One Hundred Years of Banking in the East* (London: Routledge & Kegan Paul, 1954); and Maurice Collis, *Wayfoong: The Hongkong and Shanghai Banking Corporation* (London: Faber & Faber, 1965).

34. U.S. Department of Commerce and Labor, Bureau of Corporations, *The International Harvester Co.: March 3, 1913* (Washington, D.C.: Government Printing Office, 1913), 1-30, 149-50, 166; "Statement of Hemp Exports, Fiscal Year 1911," U.S. National Archives, Bureau of Insular Affairs, Record Group 350, entry 845-123.

35. James H. Blount, *The American Occupation of the Philippines, 1898-1912* (1912; reprint, Quezon City: Malaya Books, 1968), 604-22; Pomeroy, *American Neo-Colonialism*, 175-77. The annual *Report of the Philippine Commission* regularly included a request for repeal of this legislation. See also the writings of such colonial officials as W. Cameron Forbes and Charles Burke Elliott. Dean C. Worcester, as usual, ran counter to his colleagues.

36. Theobald Diehl (Special Commissioner, Bureau of Customs, Philippines) to Clarence R. Edwards (Chief, U.S. Bureau of Insular Affairs), 8 Aug. 1911, U.S. National Archives, Bureau of Insular Affairs,

Record Group 350, entry 845-117; Blount, *American Occupation*, 611-12; Hugo H. Miller, assisted by Charles H. Storms, *Economic Conditions in the Philippines* (Boston: Ginn & Co., 1913), 73-76; Keith Hartman, "The Henequen Empire in Yucatan: 1870-1910" (Master's thesis, University of Iowa, 1966), 194-98, 214-15.

37. Irvine H. Anderson, Jr., *The Standard-Vacuum Oil Company and United States East Asian Policy, 1933-1941* (Princeton: Princeton University Press, 1975), 202-220; Gleeck, *American Business*, 15-20; *The Petroleum Almanac* (New York: National Industrial Conference Board, 1946), 342-46; *Moody's Manual, 1941*; Richard Hooley and Vernon W. Ruttan, "The Philippines," in *Agricultural Development in Asia*, ed. R. T. Shand (Berkeley: University of California Press, 1969), 215-17.

38. Harold C. Livesay, "The Ford Motor Company in the Philippines," seminar presentation, University of Michigan, 30 Nov. 1979; Livesay to author, 9 May 1980.

39. Anderson, *Standard Vacuum*, 214; Jenkins, *American Economic Policy*, 42-51; Hartendorp, *History of Industry*, 153-62; Abaya, *Betrayal*, 200-201; Gleeck, *American Business*, 18, 106-10.

40. *Philippine Liberation Courier*, 23 Feb. 1979; *Philippine Times*, 17-23 Mar. 1979; Livesay, "The Ford Motor Company." Allegations of corruption also surrounded the Westinghouse contract for a nuclear reactor in the Philippines; see *Philippine Times*, 31 Jan. 1978ff., and *Philippine Liberation Courier*, 10 Feb. 1978ff., which reprint or summarize major wire service reports.

41. Such restrictions have been imposed not only by the Republic of the Philippines (particularly in the late 1950s and 1960s), but also by Spain (in the 1890s) and Japan (in the 1940s), each favoring its own interests over those of foreign rivals. Had any of these efforts

been longer-lived, the course of Philippine-American relations might have been very different.

42. Jim Morrell, "Aid to the Philippines: Who Benefits?," *International Policy Report* 5 (October 1979):1-16; *Philippine Liberation Courier*, 20 Mar. 1980. For an effort to look at levels of living in one region over the last 150 years of colonialism, see Owen, *Prosperity Without Progress*. Shalom, *United States and the Philippines: Neocolonialism*, 145-60, ably summarizes "The Human Costs of Neocolonialism" in the Philippines.

43. We lack sufficient reliable data to study with any precision the result of the comparably disproportionate relationship between the Soviet Union and Cuba since 1959, but it should be interesting, in time, to examine the factor of magnitude in this noncapitalist context. Certainly there are preliminary signs that it is not entirely healthy for the Cubans; whenever Moscow gets a cold, Havana sneezes.